BY NATAŠA PANTOVIĆ NUIT

Mindful Being towards Mindful Living Course

Alchemy of Love Mindfulness Training

www.artof4elements.com

Introduction to Self-Development Course Alchemy of Love

Our purpose is *to help you grow as a conscious human being*.

Understand Conscious Relationships

We hope to help you discover Your Self; inspire you to live more passionate and sensitive life; helping you listen to your Soul, finding your-own space in this matrix of life, making a genuine contribution to humanity.

So, why Self Development?

Self development is a way of Life. **Our Self Development never ends.** We are never too young or too old for personal growth.

We have an amazing potential to reach our highest potential, to have truly inspiring careers and loving relationships.

Unfortunately, often we walk through our lives asleep, we let our habits rule us, and find it difficult to change our beliefs. Recognizing the power of our Mind and the power of our Soul, learning the art of Concentration and Love, we are learning to Live with the Flow, not against it.

It is in our **nature to learn and grow**. For happiness we need to learn to Love, we need to learn to Concentrate and we should keep the flow and energy of inspiration within our lives.

Taking a commitment to grow, work on Self, spiritually develop, we **take responsibility for our lives.**

Learning the art of **Self Development** we learn about **power of mind**, **consciousness**, **mindfulness**, **true love**, and we become aware of the possibility to live life in harmony with ourselves, our family, neighbors, our relatives, our parents, animals, plants, and the planet Earth. Through a process of **self-discovery**, we will learn mindfulness, we will get in touch with conscious behavior and change our attitudes so that we are not ruled by instincts, habits and someone else's beliefs.

Our Soul is the true driver of the chariot called our body and mind, and it is a source of an amazing inner knowing.

Various self-development Transformation Tools, Activities and Workshops

Contents

Introduction to Self-Development Course Alchemy of Love 2
    Alchemy of Love Self Development Course Methodology 7
    Photos and Videos 8

Commitment Contract 12

Module 1 Body 22
    Observe Your Nutrition 23
    Personality Questionnaire 1 Your attitude towards your body 28
    Exercise 1 Defining Areas for Improvement 32
    Exercise 2 Rhythm and Food 34
    Exercise 3 Create Your Dream Healthy Menu 41
    Exercise 4 Breaking Stereotypes 43
    Exercise 5 Conscious Jog 44

Module 2 Your Home 46
    Observe Your Attitude towards your Home 47
    Questionnaire 1 Describing Your Environment 51
    Exercise 1 Defining Areas of Improvement within Your Home 54
    Exercise 3 Conscious Use of Colors 61

Module 3 Conscious & Unconscious Thinking 63
    Happiness Test, Alchemy of Love Self Development Course 65
    Questionnaire 1 Your Thinking Patterns 67
    Exercise 1: Practice Mindfulness 68
    What is Mindfulness 70
    Exercise 2: Learn How to Breath 72
    Breath is Life 72
    Exercise 3 Identify Your Mental Fixations 76
    Exercise 4 Train Your Will Power 79
    Exercise 5: Practice Concentration and Focus 81
    Exercise 6: Draw Your Mandala 84
    Task 1 Start with your Daily Meditation 89

    Human Brain and its Magic 91

    Practice Creativity 97

Module 4 Time / Life Wasters 100

    Questionnaire 1 Your Time Wasters 101

    Exercise 1: Master Your Daily Habits 104

    Human Brain and Technology 106

Module 5 Feelings 109

    Observe Your Feelings 110

    Exercise 1: Exercise Awareness 114

    Exercise 2: Your Soul's Diary 116

    Exercise 3: Practice Virtues 117

Module 6 Core Beliefs 122

    Understanding Core Beliefs 123

    Questionnaire 1 My Core Beliefs 124

    Exercise 2 Draw a Flower of Beliefs 130

    Exercise 3 My Name 131

    Our Core Beliefs Article: Clichés and myths of Sexual attractiveness 134

Module 7 Relationships 136

    Questionnaire 1 Relationship Questionnaire 137

    Exercise 2: Are You Truly Listening? 144

    Exercise 3 Exercise Conscious Speech 146

    Exercise 4: Circle of Love 148

    Exercise 5: Your Relationship Plan 150

    Relationships Article: Chemistry of Love: Is true love forever 153

    Exercise 6: Express Freedom 155

    Exercise 7: Express Love 155

    Sex and Long Term Relationships - Why do we stop having sex? 156

    Sexual Evolution: Cultural Revolution that is still to happen 159

    Relationship and Sexual Hygiene 161

Module 8 Our Greater Surrounding 164

    Questionnaire 1 Our Greater Surrounding 165

    Exercise 1 Change the Word 168

Exercise 2 I have the power to change the world...169

Exercise 2: Service..170

Module 9 Your Dreams... 171

Exercise 1 Identify Your True Dreams...173

Questionnaire 1 Your True Dreams...176

Exercise 1 Your Personal Development Plan..185

What is Karma?..190

Exercise 1 So What is Karma For You?...190

Exercise 2: Your Spiritual Diary...191

Exercise 3 Drumming, Meditation, Yoga Circle..196

 Exercise 1 Have Divine as the main focus all through your day..198

Exercise 2 Enter Your Dream World..199

Exercise 3 Seek Spiritual Company...201

List of Recommended Books..202

ALCHEMY OF LOVE SELF DEVELOPMENT COURSE METHODOLOGY

BALANCING FOUR ELEMENTS

The four elements within each one of us are: air, earth, fire, and water, four states of matter Life chooses to manifest on Earth: Jung describes them as four basic components of a personality: **intuition, sensation, thinking and feeling**.

In an attempt to deeper explore the infinite game of Life, together with you, we will explore:

- **Earth** that is fixed, rigid, static and quiet, and symbolizes your **world of senses**;

- **Water** that is the primordial Chaos, is fluidity and flexibility, and symbolizes your **subconscious mind**; **Intuition** is a deeper perception. Without clear evidence or proof, intuition perceives the subtle inner relationships and underlying processes creatively, and imaginatively.

- **Fire** that is boundless and invisible, and is a parching heat that consumes all, or within its highest manifestation, becomes the expression of Divine Love. It is a **symbol of your emotions**, and

- **Air** that has no shape and is incapable of any fixed form. It symbolizes **your world of thoughts**. It is a rational, systematic process, it is our intellectual comprehension of things.

All elements are bound by:

- **Soul** that stands at the center of the four elements as an Essence, an Observer, Consciousness coming forth to **experience the magic of Life**.

Taoists with their concept of Yin and Yang, Yogis with their belief in two opposite energy forces that flow through our body (Ida and Pingala), Jung that arranges the four functions (intuition, thinking, emotions, sensation) into two pairs of opposites – sensations / intuition and thinking / feeling that form our personality;

PHOTOS AND VIDEOS

Photos and Videos could be a wonderful tool that will increase your self-awareness and inspire your self improvement journey. We encourage you to make a video of your Journey from Week 1 to Week 12 of the Course. You could record inspiring moments, quotes that intrigued you, poems that you've created, people that gave you strength during this journey, messages that you've received from Divine through the books, through the synchronicity, all through your day.

If you are using photos, you could photograph your particular habit / state of body / state of your home, etc. during Week 1 / Week 6 / Week 12 of the course. This will give you a wonderful collage that will remind you of this little Journey of Self Discovery.

If you have a video and want to share it with others, create a 10min version, and send it to us, because this will be a way to spread your inspiration further and the way to learn from you. And remember: **ENJOY YOUR JOURNEY**!

Individual or Group Work

You could be following this course individually, with your friend or a partner, or in a group. While individual work gives you all the freedom you want to adapt the exercises to your own needs, the group work will give you inspiration and steady flow.

If you work as an individual you will be tempted to rush through the exercises, go to the next questionnaire without following the instructions for the week, reduce the time you spend in self-observing, or forget about the weekly tasks. To follow the self development course properly you will have to strengthen your Will Power. Your curious self will want to rush through all the exercises, your Ego will try to 'protect' you from any changes in your life, your lazy Self will get bored practicing virtues, etc. If you are working in a group, you will be reminded to keep up the schedule and every week you will be inspired by other people's self development work.

If you are working in a group, we recommend that:

- you meet at least once a week,

- you chose a different facilitator for each week (a week before), and have a task for all to share insights, inspirations, and go deeper into the essence of each exercise during the meeting,

However rewarding a group work is, you will also find challenges while working in the group. The group work has its own dynamics and one person's agendas can ruin the self development work of the whole group. If you chose to work in a group, make sure that you are aware of the groups' dynamics and that you protect all the members from any type of 'abuse'. If you are working in a group we recommend that you set the rules at the very beginning of your self development work. The example of the rules could be:

- Honesty & Trust
- Confidentiality
- Do not share your Soul's Diary or Spiritual Diary or share just snippets or inspiration that you got from it
- Do not compete
- Respect for all

You could also set a Group Motto (for example: Reaching the Highest Potential), and the conditions of attendance. For example, if one wishes to attend the group work, s/he commits to: Openness and Trust, Truthfulness, minimum of 30min of daily mediation, Work on the Spiritual Diary, Reading of 30 pages of spiritual literature a week, work on Unconditional Love, etc.

The main tools we will be using within Alchemy of Love Course are:

Title	Description of Transfrmation Tools
MODULE 1 Attitude towards Body	We will help you examine your body, your health, your exercise regime, the food that you eat, your habits and patterns.
MODULE 2, Attitude towards Home	We will help you examine your home, the environment that surrounds you, your habits and patterns.
MODULE 3, Thinking Patterns	Examine your Mind and your every-day thoughts. Look into your conscious and sub-conscious addictions, identify your strengths and weaknesses.
MODULE 4, Time / Life Wasters	Often we waste time unconsciously and we need to apply a conscious effort to record this time and activities, so that we become aware of the wasters of our life
Module 5, FREE MIND: Your Feelings	We will help you examine your world of feelings and emotions.
Module 6, Your Core Beliefs	Your enemy within are your core negative beliefs. Negative beliefs hide from the consciousness and they get exposed by the magic of mindfulness and awareness.
Module 7, Relationships	We will help you examine your relationships, your **ability to love** and tune into your-own and other people's wants and needs
Module 8, Your Greater Surrounding	We live in our Greater Surrounding. Our capability for love grows and expands into our surroundings – Earth, animals, plants, our neighbors, strangers…
Module 9, Your Dreams	Turn away from your dream and it will come back to you. **Follow your dream** and it will give you a **tremendous amount of pleasure and learning**.
Module 10, Your True Goals	Identify your **True Goals** and Actions to achieve them… **Listen to your Heart and follow your Mind**!
Module 11, Spirituality	What is Spirituality for you? Start your **Spiritual Diary** and get inspired within your Spiritual Journey
Module 12, Your Spiritual Journey	Meditate, start your **Dreams Diary**, Read Spiritual Books, Seek Spiritual Company…

ALL THROUGHOUT THE EXERCISES YOU WILL BE EXPLORING:

Concentration: Learn the art of concentration and practice with your children 'focus' that will help you grow and do your day-to-day duties the best you can.

Will-Power: Work with the magic of discipline to create the life you desire

Love: Improve your ability to connect with yourself and others

Creative Intelligence: Live authentically, and express your creativity

Listen to Your Soul: Learn how to listen to your Soul' Whispers

Oneness: Realise that we are all One

Spirituality: Raise your awareness and live more consciously

We will help you look at:

- Your habits, stereotypical behaviors, prejudices
- Your dreams, & goals
- Listen to your Soul:
    - Learn Meditation & Mindfulness
    - Increasing Your capability to Love, Stay Inspired, Creative and Full of Energy
    - Using Your Soul's Diary & Spiritual Diary

Commitment Contract

Personal development **is never ending work.** It takes commitment and patience. If you are serious about personal growth, we will be more than happy to share what we know with you.

Commitment Contract

I _____

Undertake to work on my self-development during the next 12 weeks.

I commit to honestly and truthfully face my habits and beliefs, so that I can transform them into inspiring and enriching daily routines, and life-changing attitudes.

My intention is to discover and live my highest potential working with my body, mind and soul.

During these 12 weeks I commit to take care of my body giving it the adequate sleep, proper diet, and exercise. I will do my best to limit or avoid consumption of alcohol, drugs, cigarettes, and medications for the duration of the course.

I also commit to listen to my Soul's Whispers exercising daily meditation, writing Spiritual Diary, and creating my-own rituals for accessing the Power of Soul (contact with nature, music, dance, laughter, etc.).

I commit to experimenting, enjoying and exploring!

Let my Soul and Mind stay Inspired!

_____ (signature)

_____ (date)

YOUR CIRCLE OF LIFE

To understand the magic of prioritizing we will start with a practical exercise that will give you an insight about the way you spend your time...

YOUR CIRCLE OF 24 HOURS ACTIVITIES

Draw the circle of your activities during 24 hours.

If you think that you can remember, draw the circle of your activities immediately. But if in any doubt, just spend a day observing yourself: how much time did I watch TV, spend on Facebook, play Games, sleep, eat, play?

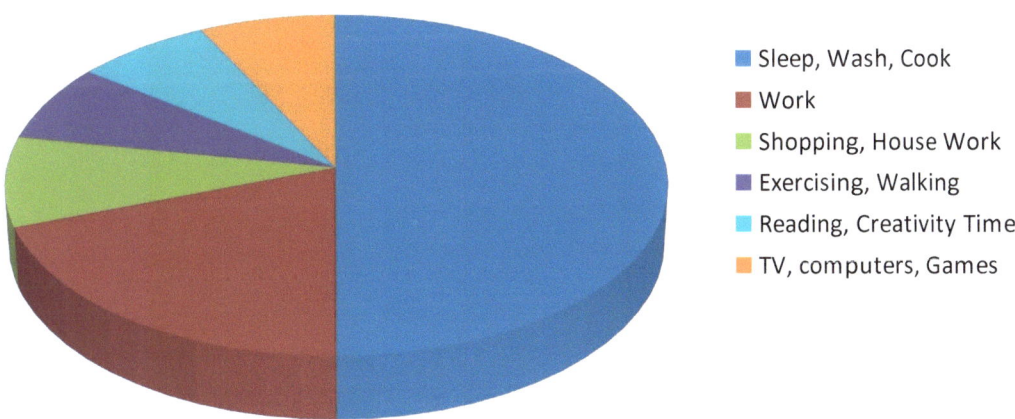

Now, analyze the list. Analyze your chart.

Take a colorful marker and highlight areas that you need to protect, activities that just MUST take place, so that you restore your inner happiness.

When you look at your day, observe the time you've spent on your own, the time you spent with your partner, with your children alone, the time you spent with your friends, and the time you spent with strangers. Create the balance within these activities, the balance of your relationships interactions.

THERE SHOULD BE A SUBTLE BALANCE BETWEEN TIME SPENT INDOORS AND TIME SPENT OUTDOORS

THERE SHOULD BE A BALANCE BETWEEN TIME SPENT ALONE AND TIME SPENT WITH FRIENDS

THERE SHOULD EXIST A BALANCE AROUND TIME SPENT IN A STRUCTURED ACTIVITY AND TIME SPENT IN FREE PLAY

Areas to Protect:	Me	My Partner	My Child
Family Meal	√		
Creativity Time	√		√
Free Play, Free Time			√
Study Time			
Friends Time			
Silent Time or Time on my own		√	
Quality Time with my Partner, Kids	√	√	√

In the evening the next day, write down your protected areas and how did you take care of them today:

- Did you skip a meal?
- Did you eat on the go?
- Did you have time for art and music?
- Did you go for your daily walk?
- Did you forget to do something that you have promised to yourself ages ago?

If you have, write down briefly what are you going to do tomorrow, what are you going to do better, what are you going to do different?

Have in mind that children will not help you with the rhythm, they will try to break it apart, it is you who needs to train it and implement it within your lives.

Your Circle of Activities during 1 week

Draw the circle of your activities during 1 week.

- Time to work / go to school
- Time for house chores: washing clothes, cleaning the house
- Time to rest / be together as a family
- Structured time for various activities (basketball, music lessons, sport)
- Free time for unstructured activities
- Time for art and music (crafts morning, music afternoon, theatre evening)
- Time for friends (one or two days for meeting friends)
- Time for the family activity (family outing) with friends
- Time for the family activity (family outing) without friends

Observe and analyze the charts

Do not clutter your time with too many activities.

Activity after activity can cause unnecessary stress and hyperactivity with children.

Draw Your Last Week Activity Schedule:

MONDAY	SCHOOL			FAMILY DINNER	
TUESDAY	SCHOOL		SPORT		EVENING OUT
WEDNESDAY	SCHOOL	LUNCH OUT WITH KIDS	MUSIC TIME	FAMILY DINNER	
THURSDAY	SCHOOL		SPORT	FAMILY DINNER	
FRIDAY	SCHOOL		COMPUTER TIME, GAMES, OR A FILM	FAMILY DINNER	
SATURDAY	BASKETBALL	MUSIC LESSON	FRIENDS		EVENING OUT
SUNDAY	FAMILY DAY		SPORT	FAMILY DINNER	

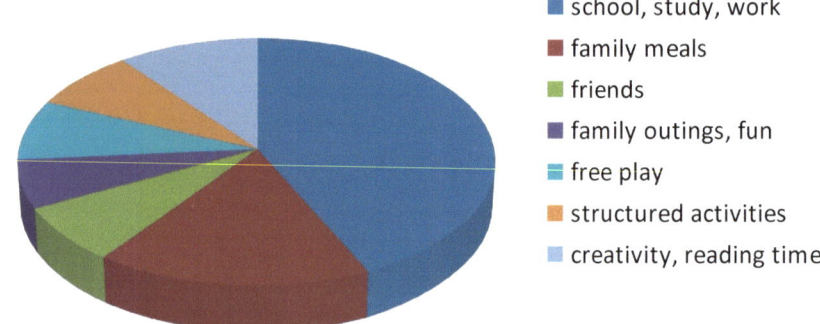

OBSERVE THE CHARTS. IS THERE ANYTHING THAT YOU CAN LEARN FROM THEM?

OBSERVE THE TIME WASTERS, BECOME CONSCIOUS OF THEM.

- How much time do you spend watching TV, on the computer, playing games?
- Do you have enough time on your own?
- Do you have enough creative time?
- Do you spend enough time with friends?

DRAW THE CIRCLE OF ACTIVITIES WITHIN YOUR IDEAL LIFE

Within the circle, you can include anything that inspires you that makes you feel good, that you aspire to. Don't forget to include the following areas:

- Your healthy body including proper rest, exercise, preparation of healthy food, etc.
- An area that says friends, and relationship with friends;
- Time spent with your loved ones: partner, parents, sister, etc.
- An area with your ideal work;

- Meditation, walks, dance, poetry, reading, your spiritual methods and tools (meditation, prayer, etc.)
- An area for pleasure, travel and adventure.

Look at it and meditate on it. This pie will later help you define goals within your life.

BE MINDFUL

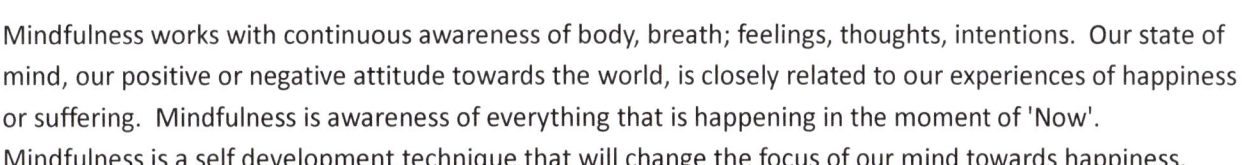

Mindfulness works with continuous awareness of body, breath; feelings, thoughts, intentions. Our state of mind, our positive or negative attitude towards the world, is closely related to our experiences of happiness or suffering. Mindfulness is awareness of everything that is happening in the moment of 'Now'. Mindfulness is a self development technique that will change the focus of our mind towards happiness.

Mindfulness is continuous undisturbed awareness of the present moment. Fully aware of here, and now, we pay attention to what is happening right in front of us, we set aside our mental and emotional baggage. To be mindful we have to re-train our mind.

Our mind is constantly busy with thoughts and feeling about our past, present and future. To stop it from useless constant chat, we must learn how to hear this noise, how to become aware of it, and to transform it through concentration into mindfulness.

We train ourselves all through our life to waste energy following our inner narratives. We are often unconsciously driven by our fears, worries and fantasies. We interpret, speculate, and project the words, thoughts and emotions around us. We should enter a space of awareness of our present moment with no emotional filters, no regrets of the past or hopes for the future, with no daydreaming and no nightmares. An ability to concentrate will give us an ability to transform a mundane situation into a very special one.

With 70,000 thoughts a day and 95% of our activity controlled by the subconscious mind, no wonder that it feels as though we are asleep most of the time. To awake, we need to train self-remembering and mindfulness. Self-remembering is an attempt to be more conscious, and more aware. It is a form of active meditation were we work to be aware of ourselves and our environment through self-remembering. The essence of the Self-Remembering technique is that while we are doing anything: reading, singing, talking, tasting, we must be aware of the Self who is reading, singing, talking or tasting.

Mindfulness increases the awareness of the nature of the mind. If we learn to control our mind and listen to our souls we can consciously choose to be joyful instead of sad, peaceful and loving, alert and relaxed...

Being mindful of our feelings we will get Delighted. The quality of life is in proportion of our capacity to get delighted. The capacity for delight is within our capacity to pay attention to things around us. Pay attention to birds singing, to clouds formations, to flowers greeting you, to kids laughing, to a beautiful person that have just passed by. Be aware of synchronicity among all living beings and be alert for the presence of Divine in All.

WHAT IS UNCONDITIONAL LOVE?

LOVE AND HAPPINESS

The essence of this wonderful feeling, this joyful state of being is that Love can and must be trained! To choose Happiness as the way of Life, one needs to train Love The Soul that chose the path of developing the virtues becomes intoxicated with good qualities, and it starts fully and deeply loving and trusting, living within this space of openness, living within the space of Being Love.

FALLING IN LOVE

Professor Arthur Arun, the New York psychologist, studied the dynamics of what happens when people fall in love and within his experiment he asked complete strangers to spend around half an hour together, to share intimate details of their lives with each other, and they were asked to stare into each others eyes for a few minutes, silently. As a result of this experiment, many couples reported that they felt a strong attraction / falling in love for each other and two of them even got married.

WHAT IS LOVE?

So, what do you think? **What is love**? If we enter the space of **openness** and **trust**, can we **fall in love** with a complete stranger? If you have experienced love, you will agree with me that being loved and loving fills us with a warm, secure, floating feeling. **Living love**, we start listening to our inner-most being, and we chose to be happy.. Touched by the Love Magic we open, and dissolve our boundaries. However, the Cupid's arrow also carries jealousy, it exposes us to our ugly side, working with our sub-consciousness fears...

Our philosophers, our poets, our scientists, tell us that the formula of our Universe is Love, governed by Venus. She combines the highest spiritual with the lowest material qualities - Love materialised on Earth. She is born in water, from mud, and she bears the lotus. Her mystical mantra is: 'Love is the law, but Love controlled by Will'.

Love needs to become a Conscious Effort, Love needs to be Trained

The love parents feel for their children, the love between partners, the love for friends are all wonderful exercises for worshipers of Love. When in love, we have a tendency to exaggerate small positive qualities or not to see negative ones, getting disappointed when we 'fall-out' of love and open our eyes to all the partner's vices. Love needs to enter our daily meditations, become our guide, and become part of our being.

'Our philosophers, our poets, our scientists, tell us that the **Formula of our Universe is Love** governed by **Venus**. She combines the **highest spiritual** with the **lowest material** qualities: **Love** materialised on **Earth**. She is born in water, from mud, & she bears the lotus. Her **mystical mantra** is: **'Love is the Law, but Love controlled by Will'**.

Mindful Being
by Nuit

www.artof4elements.com

Unconditional Love

'No matter how new the face or how different the dress and behavior, there is no significant division between us and other people. It is foolish to dwell on external differences, because our basic natures are the same. Ultimately, humanity is one and this small planet is our only home, If we are to protect this home of ours, each of us needs to experience a vivid sense of universal altruism. It is only this feeling that can remove the self-centered motives that cause people to deceive and misuse one another.' **Dalai Lama**

TRANSFORMATION TOOLS, ALCHEMY OF LOVE

MODULE 1 BODY

Module 1: We will help you examine your body, your health, the food that you eat, your habits and patterns.

Our purpose is *to help you grow as a Conscious Human Being*.

OBSERVE YOUR NUTRITION

We highly recommend that you spend the first 4 days in measuring your time spent in exercising, resting, and observing your eating and drinking habits. We are often too tired to consciously observe our eating and drinking patents. Also we often do not remember the truth and we need to make a conscious effort to record our habits so that we can become aware of them. It is the best if your partner is also following the program so that you can inspire each other and grow together.

DAY 1 TO 4 LET'S LOOK AT YOUR DRINKING HABITS...

Observe your habits in respect to drinking. Take a note-book with you and jot down all the liquids that you in-take during the first four days. Do not consciously or sub-consciously obstruct your usual habits. This exercise is designed to raise your awareness around drinking.

Day 1 to 4	Your Drinking Habits	Day 1	Day 2	Day 3	Day 4	Quality (1-5)	Quantity (1-5)
	Drinking water	IIII	4 (glasses)			3	3
	Drinking juices		1	1	2		
	Drinking non caffeinated tea	3	1				
	Drinking caffeinated tea	1	1				
	Drinking milk	1					
	Hot chocolate, milk-shake, etc.		1				
	Drinking coffee	1	2				
	Wine, beer, liquids, Other	1				3	3

Note: I is 1 unit: 2dl of water, 1 cup of tea, 1 espresso, 1dl of wine, etc

ALCHEMY OF LOVE COURSE   MODULE 1 MINDFUL EATING   OBSERVATION EXERCISE 1

Date_____   Name_____

Day 1 to 4	Your Drinking Habits	Day 1	Day 2	Day 3	Day 4	Quality (1-5)	Quantity (1-5)
	Water						
	Milk						
	Freshly squeezed fresh fruit, veggies						
	Herbal non caffeinated tea						
	Caffeinated tea						
	Packed juices or fizzy drinks						
	Hot chocolate, milk-shake, etc.						
	Coffee						
	Wine, beer, liquids						
	Other						

Note: I is 1 unit: 2dl of water, 1 cup of tea, 1 espresso, 1dl of wine, etc

Your Notes:

_____
_____

Mindful Eating   by Nuit

We do food every single day. **Conscious Eating** is a big step toward **Conscious Living**. Quality and Quantity of Food is directly related to our **Health and State of Mind**. We can use food to help us **recover** from **Stress and Disease**. Not taking food seriously will eventually lead to Stress or Disease

With Delicious RAW VEGAN RECIPES
www.artof4elements.com

DAY 1 TO 4 LET'S LOOK AT YOUR **EATING HABITS**

Observe your habits in respect to food. Take a note-book with you and jot down all the food items that you in-take during the day. Do not consciously or sub-consciously obstruct your usual habits. This exercise is designed to raise your awareness around eating.

Day 1 to 4	Your Eating Habits	Day 1	Day 2	Day 3	Day 4	Quality (1-5)	Quantity (1-5)
	Breakfast (quality)	- muesli - fruit - yogurt				Your mark for quality	Your mark for quantity
	Lunch	- toast & salad					
	Dinner	- rice - veggies					
	Snaking	- crisp - croissant - apple					
	Over-eating	Y for dinner					
	Fresh Fruit	1 apple					
	Fresh Vegetables	Veggie Soup					
	Organic	(Y/N) ✓					
	Seasonal, Local	(Y/N) ✓					

Page 25

ALCHEMY OF LOVE COURSE MODULE 1 MINDFUL EATING OBSERVATION EXERCISE 2

Date_____ Name_____

Your Eating Habits	Day 1	Day 2	Day 3	Day 4	Qlty (1-5)	Qnty (1-5)
Breakfast						
Lunch						
Dinner						
Snaking						
Over-eating						
Fresh Fruit						
Fresh Veggies						
Organic						
Seasonal, Local						
Frozen, Canned						
Junk Food						
Hidden sugars						
Sweets, obvious sugars						
Sit down to eat						
Restaurant or Home Made						
Carbohydrate overdose						
Meat overdose						

Your Notes:

Your Overall Mark for the Day					
Your drinking and eating quality and quantity analysis	1	2	3	4	5

At the end of your observation, you will be able to produce the following table:

Balanced and healthy diet	Day 1	Day 2	Day 3	Day 4
I have a balanced and healthy diet, I eat lots of fresh greens and veggies				
My child has a balanced and healthy diet, s/he eats lots of fresh greens and veggies				
My partner has a balanced and healthy diet, eats lots of fresh greens and veggies				
I drink healthy, I take enough water and my water is of good quality				
My child's drinking patterns are healthy. S/he drinks enough water and his/her water is of good quality.				
My partner drinks healthy, taking enough water and water is of good quality				

At the end of the observation period, we will work with a questionnaire that highlights your habits, patterns, re-occurring problems.

Have in mind that this questionnaire is YOURS.

Add any question that you feel is more relevant for your life.

Be truthful and honest and your Soul will rejoice!

PERSONALITY QUESTIONNAIRE 1 YOUR ATTITUDE TOWARDS YOUR BODY

ANSWER THE FOLLOWING PERSONALITY QUESTIONS RELATED TO YOUR NUTRITION, HEALTH AND BODY

Read each sentence and rate them from 1 (really bad) to 5 (I am super happy with it).

Answer to what extent you feel this statement is true.

My Body Questionnaire	1	2	3	4	5
I drink enough water and my water is of good quality		√			
I have a balanced and healthy diet, I eat lots of fresh greens and veggies			√		
I do not over-eat, I am happy with my weight				√	
My energy levels are high				√	
My sleep is of good quality and I am happy with its quantity				√	
I exercise regularly: I walk, roller-blade, swim, run at least three times per week			√		
My caffeine intake is healthy		√			
I rarely drink alcohol				√	
I do not use drugs					√

WRITE THE ANSWERS OF THE PERSONALITY QUESTIONNAIRE

After you have answered your questions, meditate on the answers and where the problems within your life might be.

Use a colored marker to highlight areas that might need improvement. Add whatever you feel is missed out from this list. The ranking from 1 to 5 will indicate your list of priorities.

Mindful Eating by Nuit

We are all children that need **nurturing**, **love** and **care**. So give your **inner child** that nurturing and love, give yourself back the **joy of preparing healthy and nutritious meals**, joy of experiencing food without TV, reading, working, rush.

with Delicious RAW VEGAN RECIPES
www.artof4elements.com

ALCHEMY OF LOVE COURSE　　　MODULE 1 MINDFUL EATING　　QUESTIONNAIRE 1

Date_____　　　　Name_____

	My Body Questionnaire	1	2	3	4	5
1	I drink enough water and my water is of good quality					
2	I have a balanced and healthy diet, I eat lots of fresh greens and veggies					
3	I do not over-eat, I am happy with my weight					
4	My energy levels are high					
5	My sleep is of good quality and I am happy with its quantity					
6	I exercise regularly: I walk, roller-blade, swim, run at least three times per week					
7	My caffeine intake is healthy					
8	I rarely drink alcohol					
9	I do not use drugs					
10	I do not smoke					
11	I do not use medication					

12	I do not use sugars excessively / soft-drinks / food items loaded with sugar				
13	I do not eat junk food, use refined salt or food items loaded with salt				
14	I spend every day in Nature				
15	I spend enough time on-my-own meditating / contemplating / Being				
16					
17					

My List of Priorities:
Items Marked as 1, 2 and 3 are:

My Body Questionnaire	1	2	3

EXERCISE 1 DEFINING AREAS FOR IMPROVEMENT

Study each answer that you are not happy with and determine what precise action you would like to do to change your state of body, mind, emotions.

Write down the areas that need improvement. Be specific...

For Example:

My Body feels depleted of energy			
Because of:	**Action Items:**	**What stops you from doing it?**	**Any alternative?**
My lousy posture	Do some Pilates to strengthen your spine	Hate Pilates	Try Yoga
My food allergies	Visit the doctor to determine the list of food	Hate doctors	Try alternative methods – muscle testing, etc.
A cough that won't leave	A doctor / A herbalist	My cough is not serious enough just annoying	More tea, care, lemon & honey, more rest
Not getting enough sleep	My bed is not firm enough	Never got to buying a new one	Let's do it than!

Often, we guess the solution of our problem but our habitual-mind-set invents a valid reason against the improvement. So that is why our list of action has a column called: Alternatives. There are always alternatives that will help your condition and are difficult to refuse...

ALCHEMY OF LOVE COURSE   MODULE 1 MINDFUL EATING   EXERCISE 1

Date_____   Name_____

Defining Areas of Improvement 1:			
Because of:	Action Items:	What stops you from doing it?	Any alternative?

Also write the action items that you would like to pursue, so that these conditions change.

Defining Areas of Improvement 2:			
Because of:	Action Items:	What stops you from doing it?	Any alternative?

EXERCISE 2 RHYTHM AND FOOD

If you have a problem with over-eating, eating too often, eating too little, eating junk food, food allergies, etc. you need to become aware and conscious of your body / mind reactions to food.

EXERCISE 2A RE-CREATE THE ROUTINE AROUND YOUR FOOD

- Eat around the table.
- Eat at set times.
- Eat with no distractions

We are all children that need nurturing, love and care. So give your inner child that nurturing and love, give yourself back the joy of preparing healthy and nutritious meals... Re-create the routine around your food: eat around the table, eat at the set times, don't skip your meals.

When you eat, just eat, do not do anything else. Do not read or watch news, use this time to become conscious of quality and quantity of food that you are taking. Your enjoyment will multiply and fulfillment soon follow. The quality will replace the quantity, awareness will become your guide and protector.

Taste your healthy and nutritious meals without external interruptions, experience the joy of tasting food without TV, reading, working, rush, mobile, messaging, etc... Savor and enjoy your food while eating, become 'mindful' of your food, rather than just swallowing your food while watching TV, surfing the Net, or reading the paper.

Mindful Eating   by Nuit

Real Food is not GMO modified, has no poisons, no preservatives, no coloring's **Real Food** is **Fruit** and **Veggies** that are seasonal & local. **Real Food** is **not processed, frozen, or prep-packaged** Whole, unprocessed foods are much healthier.

with Delicious RAW VEGAN RECIPES
www.artof4elements.com

Exercise 2B Chose your Food Mindfully

SWAP
- meat for veggies
- soft drinks for spring water (with a bit of lemon)
- packed & processed foods with organics
- sugar with honey or fruits
- milk-chocolate bar for a piece of dark chocolate
- a handful of sweets for a handful of berries
- an apple pie for a baked apple
- cream for plain yoghurt
- 2nd cup of coffee for a cup of white or green tea

www.artof4elements.com

- swap meat for veggies

- swap white for brown

- swap soft drinks for spring water (with a bit of lemon or lime)

- swap colored and processed food with organics

- swap sugar with honey or fruits

- swap a milk-chocolate bar for a piece of dark chocolate

- swap a handful of sweets for a handful of berries

- swap an apple pie for a baked apple

- swap cream for plain yoghurt

- swap 2nd cup of coffee for a cup of white or green tea

Become conscious of quality and quantity of food that you are taking.

Let it be fresh, organic, locally grown, seasonal, nutritious, use non-processed whole-meal items, and lots of raw veggies. Let the quality of your food items replace the quantity, and allow the food awareness to become your guide.

With the awareness you will start respecting yourself and the enjoyment will multiply.

Mindful Eating   by Nuit

Empower your **Physical Body**, helping your **Mind** and **Soul**:
1. Chose **Healthy Food**
2. Create **Daily Routine** with **Nutritional Habits**
3. Eat **Mindfully** practicing **Mindfulness & Willpower Exercises**

with Delicious RAW VEGAN RECIPES
www.artof4elements.com

EAT LOTS OF FRUIT AND VEGGIES

Fruit have their best healing and nutrition effects when eaten separately from grains and vegetables. Eat fruits one hour before consuming any other foods and the best time is MORNING.

Nothing else can replace or substitute fruits and vegetables in our diet. Fruits and vegetables provide the body with our #1 source of antioxidants, vitamins and minerals.

Maintaining good health requires balancing the alkaline and acidic level of your blood through your nutrition and your lifestyle choices. The way certain foods are chosen and prepared can change how healthy they are for us. Let it be fresh, healthy, without preservatives, suitable for you. Let it be tasty and looking wonderful.

Mindful Eating   by Nuit

We do food every single day. **Conscious Eating** is a big step toward **Conscious Living**. Quality and Quantity of Food is directly related to our **Health and State of Mind**. We can use food to help us **recover** from **Stress and Disease**. Not taking food seriously will eventually lead to Stress or Disease

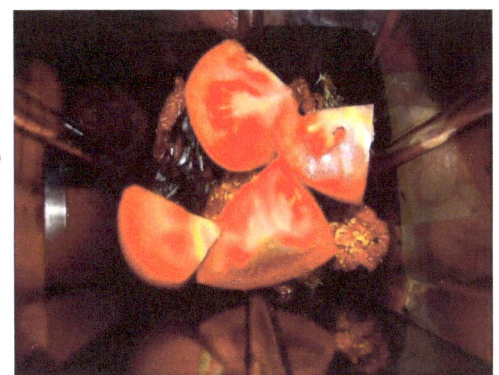

With Delicious RAW VEGAN RECIPES
www.artof4elements.com

EXERCISE 2C EAT MINDFULLY

Be aware of that sensation of chewing and somewhere in the middle of the bite, stop for a moment, to again experience the battle of senses that occurs when we are eating.

1. Decorate Your Table

Preparing food could be an art form, a very beautiful one! So, decorate your table. Arrange your food using your nicest plates, light a candle and place a flower arrangement on your table as though you are serving a guest!

2. Start eating after a short meditation or prayer

This will make you face the animal instinct of HUNGER, and you will turn again towards Peace.

Just before you take your first bite, sit in front of your food for a minute or two before eating. You may wish to close your eyes. Respecting the food, the space around you, the silence, will make you face your animal instinct of HUNGER, relax you, and you will turn towards food peacefully.

3. **Stay with this instinct to swallow**

Keep the food in your mouth for some time and observe the instinct to take more than it is really necessary, to gulp the food. We are practicing awareness. We want the process of food consumption to enter into our **awareness**.

We want to be aware of what we are eating, aware of our addictions, aware of our animal instincts. When under the light of consciousness these instincts become weaker and we can use them for more pleasure, instead of suffering within our sense of greed.

4. **Eat Your Meal Mindfully**

Eat slowly, chew properly, lift your fork gradually and thoughtfully, experiencing every movement fully. After finishing your meal, take a few moments to notice that you have finished.

Allow the feeling of gratitude to fill your mind, you just had this wonderful nourishing meal to support you on your further journey.

5. **Stop eating just before you are full**

If we over-eat, we feel drowsy, we are not fully active, If we leave the table a little hungry, we feel much more energized later on.

6. **Taste a wide range of food items**

Try sweet and sour foods, liquids and solids, hot and cold foods. Before you eat, smell your food, as though you are experiencing the finest wine, stay with each experience.

7. **Enjoy Your Meal!**

Mindful Eating   by Nuit

'Lot of us have Problems with **over-eating**, eating too often, too little, **eating junk food**, food allergies... **Mindfulness** of our **relationship to food** gives us an **Awareness** of the **Body Mind Soul** re-action & connection to food.'

with Delicious RAW VEGAN RECIPES
www.artof4elements.com

EXERCISE 3 CREATE YOUR DREAM HEALTHY MENU

EXERCISES FOR RAISING AWARENESS AROUND FOOD: HEALTHY VEGETARIAN MEAL PLAN

Create your-own healthy vegetarian meal plan for a week. Try it out for a week!

An example of a healthy vegetarian meal plan would look like this:

	Breakfast	Lunch	Snacks	Dinner
Monday	Quinoa with Strawberries, Coconut, Seeds	Spinach and Greens Salad	Popcorns	Whole Wheat Vegetable Stuffed Flatbread
Tuesday	Buckwheat Pancakes with fruits and nuts	Raw experiment: Sprouts, tomato, avocado, carrots	Fresh Seasonal Fruit + Pumpkin Seeds	Crackers with Hummus and Veggies
Wednesday	Coconut millet	Feta and Avocado Wraps	Blackberries and Walnuts	Whole Wheat Pancakes (See: Unhealthy Treats)
Thursday	Fruit feast + Green Smoothie	Roasted Vegetables with Cheese Sauce	Yogurt	Pasta with Pesto
Friday	Raw Buckwheat Porridge	See: Lunch Out	Brown Toast with Honey	Roasted Veggies and Rice

ALCHEMY OF LOVE COURSE   MODULE 1 MINDFUL EATING   EXERCISE 3 DREAM MENU

Date_____   Name_____

	Breakfast	Lunch	Snacks	Dinner
Monday				
Tuesday				
Wednesday				
Thursday				
Friday				

EXERCISE 4 BREAKING STEREOTYPES

These exercises are designed to break stereotypes that are created around the ritual of food.

- Eat at least one meal during the week with your fingers, or using a palm leaf instead of a plate, or use a branch instead of a fork, etc.

- Create your-own 'eating' ritual with flowers, candles, your meditation or a prayer.

- Whenever you can eat with your friends and/or family.

LUNCH OUT & UNHEALTHY TREATS

Our busy life-styles often force us to eat out constantly. During the Alchemy of Love Corse, chose a day or two, when you will be going out for lunch or dinner. Treat yourself to unhealthy treats, have your-own Pizza or Sweets day, but try to stick to Healthy, Fresh, Home Made during the rest of the time.

Dedicate a day within your Dream Healthy Menu for unhealthy treats: cakes, or any of your favorite indulgence. Moving this 'habit' into one day, you are leaving a space for a 'treat', you eat healthy during the week and enjoy your treat on a chosen day. Having a day for 'treats', will reduce dramatically your sugar and junk intake during the week.

EXERCISE 5 CONSCIOUS JOG

MAKE A JOG A CONSCIOUS WEEKLY EXERCISE

Sri Chinmoy (1931 – 2007), was an Indian **Spiritual Master** who began teaching meditation in the US in 1964. He taught **meditation** as a core **spiritual practice**. He also **encouraged physical fitness** and sports as a vehicle for **personal transformation**. Many of his disciples took on running marathon as a spiritual discipline.

'While you run, each breath that you take is connected with a higher reality. While you are jogging, if you are in a good **consciousness**, your breath is being blessed by a higher inner breath. Of course, while you are jogging if you are chatting with one of your friends about mundane things, then this will not apply. But if you are in a good **consciousness** while you are running, each breath will connect you with a higher, deeper, inner reality. **Running also has a special symbolic meaning. In the spiritual life, we are eternal runners, running along Eternity's Road**.'

Make jogging a conscious activity.

Always breathe through your nose.

As you start to jog feel the air move around you, feel your body tense, feel your body muscles act and re-act. Feel your chest expanding and contracting.

Follow your breathing and listen to it. If your mind wanders off, just come back to the **consciousness** of your body and to your breathing.

It's best not to push yourself too much and to run at around 70% of your pace.

Focus your attention on the physical activity, on a specific movement your body is making, how the ground feels under your feet, focus on the wind that touches your face.

The best practice for any 'mindfulness' is switching off your music while jogging and becoming 'mindful' of jogging itself.

TRANSFORMATION TOOLS ALCHEMY OF LOVE

MODULE 2 YOUR HOME

Conscious Parenting by Nuit

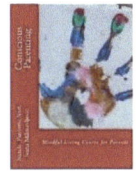

'If we wish to have a beautiful, peaceful and safe home, we need healthy expanding roots that go deep into the ground. These roots are our **Routine**, our **Stability**, our **Structure**.'

Often the environment we live in mirrors our Soul's state. If we are surrounded by Chaos, our Mind can not function Peacefully. If we love ourselves, we will give our-selves the **gift of Beauty** in everything that surrounds us, the **gift of Harmony** and the **gift of Zen Emptiness**

OBSERVE YOUR ATTITUDE TOWARDS YOUR HOME

YOUR HOME IS A PORT YOU'LL ALWAYS RETURN TO, YOUR HIDING PLACE, YOUR BASE, THE PLACE WHERE YOU TAKE REFUGE, GAIN STRENGTH, LIVE EVERY DAY.

What all of us need is a home with the corner-stone called: LOVE.

Everything starts from your home and everything ends there. If we did not develop the basic security that starts at home, we will start feeling insecure within other areas of our lives.

Transform your house into a home full of warmth that is a source of your strength.

The place you live in could become your energy sucker, because you did not pay attention to all the clutter or electrical appliances.

Observe your place.

How many unnecessary things do you have around you? How many appliances do you have in your kitchen?

How many TVs do you have and how often are they on? How does your wardrobe look like?

And what about the entrance to your place?

Or your spare room, what kind of clutter do you have there?

If you have a child, how does your child's bedroom look like? Is it appropriate for the age of your child or does it keep unnecessary 'memories' and toys of when your child was younger? How many never opened books do you have, how many never used clothes, how many never used items?

Each item carries an energy and with clutter we get overwhelmed with unnecessary energies all around us. Each item has a color and shape and with clutter our visual surrounding gets disharmonious and we disturb our concentration and attention and concentration and attention of our children.

The amount of time you spend inside your home is an indicator of how comfortable your home is. If you are constantly on the go, outside of your home, this might indicate your subconscious wish to 'escape' from home and its surroundings. Staying at home at all times, might indicate that you are afraid of the contact with other people and surroundings.

There is a subtle balance between outdoor and indoor activity that will naturally occur once we enjoy our home and once we feel love within and outside of the home.

ANSWER THE FOLLOWING PERSONALITY QUESTIONS RELATED TO YOUR HOME AND ENVIRONMENT YOU LIVE IN

Observe your environment and write down the major observation you have about the home you live in.

My Home

	Your Bedroom	Your Child's Bedroom	Your Living Area	Your Kitchen	Your Car	Your Desk	Your Dinning Table
Harmony			Too noisy				
Beauty	Beautiful				Perfect, just new		
Clutter	TV	Many toys		Too cluttered			Full of documents
Use			TV, computer, games				Working on DT
Missing		No shelves	Too noisy			No desk	
Beauty		Not decorated			Perfect, just new		

Page 47

Alchemy of Love Course   Module 2 Your Home   Observation Exercise 1

Date_____   Name_____

Observe Your Home	Entrance	Living Area	Yard
Harmony			
Beauty			
Clutter			
Use			

Observe Your Home	Child's Bedroom	Kitchen	Store Room / Cellar

Questionnaire 1 Describing Your Environment

Now, write down a list of sentences that describe your environment.

Answer to what extent you feel these statements are true. Rate your statements from 1 (really bad) to 5 (I am super happy with it)

		1	2	3	4	5
1	I designed a home that I love and that inspires me and others who visit it			√		
2	I surround myself with beauty			√		
3	My space is not clattered with books, unused boxes, sentimental items, children's toys, newspapers		√			
4	My car is clean in and out				√	
5	I live in a peaceful environment			√		
6						
7						

Write the answers of the Questionnaire

After you have answered your questions, meditate on answers and where the problems within your life might be.

Use a colored marker to highlight areas that might need improvement. Add whatever you feel is missed out from this list. The ranking from 1 to 5 will indicate your list of priorities.

ACTION ITEM FROM THE PERSONALITY QUESTIONNAIRE

Study each answer that you are not happy with and determine what precise action you would like to do to change your state of body, mind, emotions.

Write down the areas that need improvement. Be specific.

A-Ma Alchemy of Love by Nuit

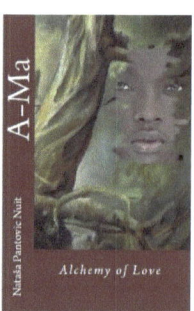

'Any substance, an **Alchemist** would tell you, is what it appears to be, set just for **a moment lost in eternity**, by parameters of a given **place**, **time**, and circumstances.

When **one** is treated with **love**, **respect** and **care**, how far can he develop?'

www.artof4elements.com

ALCHEMY OF LOVE COURSE   MODULE 2 YOUR HOME   QUESTIONNAIRE 1 DESCRIBE YOUR HOME

Date_____   Name_____

	Describe Your Home	1	2	3	4	5
1	I designed a home that I love, that inspires me & others who visit it					
2	I surround myself with beauty					
3	My space is not clattered with books, unused boxes, sentimental items, children's toys, newspapers					
4	My car is clean in and out					
5	I live in a peaceful environment					
6						
7						
8						
9						
10						

My List of Priorities:
Items Marked as 1, 2 and 3 are:

My Home Improvements	1	2	3

Page 51

Exercise 1 Defining Areas of Improvement within Your Home

Mindful Being   by Nuit

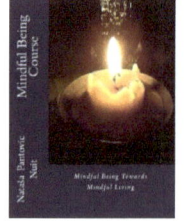

'Learning the **Art of Self Development** we learn about power of **Mind, Consciousness, Mindfulness**, **True Love**, we become aware of the possibility to **Live Life in Harmony** with ourselves, neighbors, relatives, parents, animals, plants, and the planet Earth.'

www.artof4elements.com

If your problem is your home, your car and the constant mess that follows you, be specific about it. Write down what exactly the problem is:

My space is constantly cluttered			
Because of:	**Action Items:**	**What stops you from doing it?**	**Any alternative?**
My wardrobe is full of clothes that I rarely use, my shoes are all over the place	Clear your wardrobe	I hate throwing away clothes!	Find a charity and donate them – they will appreciate it and you will start your recovery
My desks and tables are cluttered with papers, books, electronics	Clear your desks	The mess is beyond me	Mess accumulates, start by tackling a room / a desk at a time.
My pipes are leaking, my refrigerator, toaster, or hair-dryer is broken	Fix them or buy a new one	I always forget to do it	Call the plumber now!
My plants are dying	Take care of them	I have no time for plants	Find time – early morning is the best for 'plants time'
The noise level around me is constant and intolerable	Switch off TV, Radio, isolate your flat from noise	There is always something interesting ON	Have times during the day (3-4 hours without any noise around you). Practice silence.
My Storage shed is full, my spare room is full of items that I do not use	Empty / Fix / Repair	It is beyond me	Create a 'clear all' day. Fix one room at a time. Give presents from your collection, your friends will appreciate it.

I have too many appliances on the kitchen counters	Clear, remove, store	I love cooking	Give some to your mum, she will love it!
Papers and games all over the dining room table	Clear, remove, store	Children love to play games	No games at the table!
Unorganized makeup drawers	Clear, remove, store	No time	If not used or opened for centuries – remove
I have way too many never to be opened books	Clear	Love Books	Donate to a Church Fare

Now write the action items that you would like to pursue, so that these conditions change. Devote time to creating an ordered and harmonious surroundings, your Soul will love it!

ALCHEMY OF LOVE COURSE   MODULE 2 YOUR HOME   EXERCISE 1 YOUR HOME IMPROVEMENTS

Date_____   Name_____

Your Home Improvement Area:			
Because of:	**Action Items:**	**What stops you from doing it?**	**Any alternative?**

Page 54

Your Home Improvement Area:			
Because of:	Action Items:	What stops you from doing it?	Any alternative?

Write a date by which you would like to execute your action list.

Symbols & Signs → Now Imagine White Light

Let's do it! What you can do today, do not leave for tomorrow!

Action	By Date	Done √

Exercise 2: Beautify Your Home

Your Home and Beauty

Create a place where you can feel comfortable, where you can feel relaxed, where you can feel **AT HOME**.

Home is not just a place, it is a state of being

Get into a habit of lighting candles, and lighting incense. It is a wonderful habit that connects us to the energy of **Peace**.

Keep your home aired properly. **Cultivate the good quality air**. Do not smoke inside your place, and always have enough fresh air within your spaces.

Avoid air-conditioned spaces, stick to the fresh air.

Many different breathing problems are linked to air-conditioning - asthma, coughing, sneezing, itchy skin, sore nasal passages, frequent colds, frequent headaches, allergic reactions.

If you live in a climate that demands the use of air-conditioning units ($40°+$), make sure that you regularly check and clean the filters. The filters get loaded with more and more particles, reducing airflow and they become a source of air pollution itself. Keep in mind that nature has four seasons, and that we have been accustomed to live in the nature for thousands of years. **Use air-conditioned wisely, to help you live within your environment, not to rule your environment**.

Have in mind that the body experiences a certain amount of stress when it is forced to go from a boiling hot environment into a cool air of an air-conditioned room.

Keep the plants out of your bedroom - during the night they breath out Carbone dioxide that might disturb your sleep.

Exercise 3   Conscious Use of Colors

Colors vibrate, colors are alive… Use colors consciously to support you, not disturb you.

If we wish to support a particular state of being, or a particular activity, we wear or surround ourselves with a particular color.

Physical Body is represented by **RED**

Mental Body is represented by **YELLOW**

Spiritual is the color **BLUE**

Use colors consciously
Learn more about Feng Shui that uses colors in all of its recommendations.

Using color is a great way to create a peaceful feel in your spaces.

In Feng Shui, color is one of the 9 ways that you can influence your life.

Human color experiences are often cultural, however there are some universal guidelines to the way colors influence us.

Red is a physical color. Biologically red can be a signal of danger. It represents **masculine energy**. Its high vibration and strength draws attention to itself. It means energy, action, and excitement. It is often used to express sexual love.

Red, in its softer version becomes Pink, that is associated with **feminine energy**, and within its depths it hides shades of Spiritual Growth.

Blues give a quiet feeling. It creates a meditative atmosphere, relaxing tensions and refreshing the body. It is often used in bedrooms. Blues in combination with reds give violet, a colour associated with Spirit.

Orange is a color of adventure that inspires enthusiasm. It is optimistic and sociable. Orange vitalizes, inspires and encourages creativity.

Yellow is an illuminating and uplifting color. Yellow stimulates mental clarity and analytical processes. It is associated with logical reasoning and it is often used in offices. Yellow could be a warm and happy color. However, too much yellow can cause anxiety, and nervousness.

Green Green is the color of our natural environment, of growth, of plants, of spring… Add green to your spaces, add plants to your surroundings to support your growth.

Exercise 4 Implement Simple Feng Shui Tips for Your Holistic Home

- **The door and entrance** should be tidy and welcoming, *In Feng Shui* your entrance symbolizes opportunities to find you.

- *In Feng Shui*, water represents wealth and money flow. Make sure you keep the toilet seat closed, as well as the bathroom door. This will keep the wealth from flowing away from you!

- *In Feng Shui* you should not store your things under your bed. What is underneath you affects you. Clutter under the bed symbolizes subconscious blocks in your relationships. Also, never work out of your bedroom; it should only be used for rest and relaxation. Take TV, Computers, radio, mobiles out of your bedroom.

Fix what is broken (especially glass)

Throw away what is not used

Make sure that all your drains are functioning properly

Avoid Sharp angles pointing at you

Make sure all your windows are clean

Allow natural light into your spaces

Have healthy and strong plants

TRANSFORMATION TOOLS ALCHEMY OF LOVE

MODULE 3 CONSCIOUS & UNCONSCIOUS THINKING

Free Your Conscious & Sub-Conscious Mind

Our mind is constantly busy with thoughts and feelings about our past, present or future. To stop it from useless constant chat, we must learn how to hear this noise, how to become aware of it, and to transform it through **concentration into mindfulness**.

Conscious and Unconscious Thinking Process

Taoists with their concept of **Yin** (unconscious) and **Yang** (conscious force), Yogis with **Ida** and **Pingala**, that are two opposite energy forces that flow through our body, Cabbalists with the female and male side of the **Tree of Life**, all guide us towards the examination of both: our conscious mind and our or collective unconscious mind.

Researchers say that conscious mind controls our brain only 5% of the day, whereas the subconscious mind has control of our thoughts 95% of the time. A human being has 70,000 thoughts per day.

Concentration

With 70,000 thoughts a day and 95% of our activity controlled by the subconscious mind, no wonder that it feels as though we are asleep most of the time. To awake, we need to train self-remembering and mindfulness. Since, mind is in a constant movement, since thoughts attack us from everywhere, to quiet it we need to use its movement, to stop the flow of thoughts, we need to find an object of concentration and focus on it with all our might.

Unconscious or **subconscious** is vast like an ocean, and the awareness and wakefulness need to be trained for a long time. For a successful training one needs to have a strong **Will Power (willpower)**.

It is not natural to wake up at the break of dawn to meditate, and yet it is the most beautiful experience one could have. It is not natural to challenge the existing beliefs, and break the existing patterns, and yet once you manage to do it, you create space for the new patterns to form, the ones that are filled with love, acceptance, knowledge, and you give yourself a chance to spiritually grow.

HAPPINESS TEST, ALCHEMY OF LOVE SELF DEVELOPMENT COURSE

How Happy Are You?	How Happy Is Your Child / Children?	How Happy Is Your Partner?
Select one of the statements that best describes your state of happiness.		
1. In general, I am a happy person	1. In general, s/he is a happy child	1. In general, s/he is a happy person
2. I have bursts of happiness and bursts of unhappiness	2. S/he has bursts of happiness and bursts of unhappiness	2. S/he has bursts of happiness and bursts of unhappiness
3. I am neither happy nor unhappy	3. S/he is neither happy nor unhappy	3. S/he is neither happy nor unhappy
4. I feel unhappy and depressed most of the time	4. S/he feels unhappy and depressed most of the time	4. S/he feels unhappy and depressed most of the time

Now, consider your state of happiness and the % of time you feel happy, neutral or un-happy. This statement best describes me:

- \> 75% happy
- 50% neutral - 25% happy - 25% unhappy
- Neutral most of the time
- \> 75% unhappy

If your Happiness score is >75% happy and you feel most of the time happy, you are either already working on yourself or you are in love :).

If you are 50% neutral and 25% happy with 25% unhappy, you belong to most of the humanity that is labeled as 'normal'. Whether or not you chose to do this course, have in mind that happiness is a skill that could and should be trained, that love can expand beyond measure, and that living your highest potential IS very exciting and rewarding.

If you are neutral most of the time, it is time to add some flavors to your life - some spiritual strawberries and cream...

If you are > 75% unhappy and mostly feel unhappy and depressed it is the right time to take control over your life and help yourself start moving towards deeper and lasting happiness.

Learning the Art of Self Development we learn about power of mind, consciousness, mindfulness, true love, and we become aware of the possibility to live life in harmony with ourselves, our neighbors, our relatives, our parents, animals, plants, and the planet Earth. Through a process of self-discovery, we will learn mindfulness, we will get in touch with conscious behavior and change our attitudes so that we are not ruled by instincts, habits and someone else beliefs.

QUESTIONNAIRE 1 YOUR THINKING PATTERNS

We will help you examine your Mind and your every-day thoughts. We will look into your conscious and sub-conscious addictions, and we will help you identify your strengths and weaknesses.

This questionnaire contains a number of statements that describe your attitude towards your Mind.

Read each sentence and rate them from 1 (really bad) to 5 (I am super happy with it). Answer to what extent you feel this statement is true for yourself and for your child.

Your Thinking Patterns	1	2	3	4	5
I rarely watch TV					
I do not listen to music constantly					
I am not an Internet addict					
I am not a mobile addict					
I am not games / gambling addict					
I am not a workaholic					
The noise level around me is healthy					
I have an inspiring hobby					
I read inspiring books					
I have good friends and I socialize with inspiring people					
My work inspires me					
I meditate / pray / am in contact with nature regularly					

WRITE THE ANSWERS OF THE PERSONALITY QUESTIONNAIRE

After you have answered your questions, meditate on answers and where the problems within your life might be. Use a colored marker to highlight areas that might need improvement. Add whatever you feel is missed out from this list. The ranking from 1 to 5 will indicate your list of priorities.

ACTION ITEM FROM THE PERSONALITY QUESTIONNAIRE

Study each answer that you are not happy with and determine what precise action you would like to do to change your state of body, mind, emotions.

Write down the areas that need improvement.   Be specific. There are a number of mental states that evolve around your Thinking Patterns and that can potentially cause you problems. These are related to negative mental fixations that eventually end up being your emotional problems.

EXERCISE 1: PRACTICE MINDFULNESS

During this week we will also have our focus on MINDFULNESS

We eat, walk or talk but we are not aware of our-selves. If we are aware of ourselves, we are awake.

The essence of the Self-Remembering technique is that while we are doing anything – reading, singing, talking, tasting – we must be aware of the Self who is reading, singing, talking or tasting. The awareness, the energy, the life is that Self that is present within us.

In **self-remembering** there will be no thought whatever we are doing.

Walking next to the sea: the sounds are there, the wind is there, we are there with the sun, with the breeze, and with our breath and awareness of our body moving, but without our thoughts.

When eating, when bathing suddenly remember yourself, and stay as long as you can – **remembering**. Only effort is needed - a **continuous conscious** effort. Whenever you remember to do it, remember yourself.

Repeated efforts to **self-remember** lead to higher states of **consciousness** and an **awakened** state of being.

WHAT IS MINDFULNESS

SPIRITUAL WORK, MEDITATION AND MEDITATION PRACTICE

When we say *'mind'* we think of: consciousness, awareness, cognitive thinking, reasoning, perception; but also of: intuition, subconscious gibberish, or unconscious strata that influences our lives... The state of mind, our positive or negative attitude towards the world, is closely related to our experiences of happiness or suffering. The nature of mind or the matrix of various patterns that forms around our soul is closely related to the Buddhist concept of **karma**.

Mindfulness is at the heart of the Buddhist meditation. The person meditating should be **mindful** of whatever enters the mind. Silencing the internal dialogue, the meditator observes thoughts, and feelings without labeling them as good or bad.

Mindfulness works with **continuous awareness** of: the body posture and breath; of the feelings, of the mind (thoughts, intentions, images, etc.), and of the mental objects that appear during the meditation. Through bare attention, we learn to see things as they really are, without judgments and preconceptions. **Mindfulness** increases the awareness of the nature of the mind.

Mindfulness confronts us with the constant change and impermanence. The change is in the nature of life and clinging to anything will lead us to suffering. The person meditating develops the freedom to break the hold of habits.

Zen is a branch of Buddhism with special emphasis on meditation. Zen meditation, zazen, or sitting starts by focusing the awareness on the breath. During 'sitting' we close down our mental and emotional activity, and through training we develop single-pointed concentration. While meditating we work on our concentration, the rest of the day we work on mindfulness. **Mindfulness** is awareness of everything that is happening in the moment.

Mindfulness is continuous undisturbed awareness of the present moment.

Fully aware of *here*, and now, we pay attention to what is happening right in front of us, we set aside our mental and emotional baggage. To be mindful we have to re-train our mind.

We train ourselves all through our life to waste energy following our inner narratives. We are often unconsciously driven by our fears, worries and fantasies. We interpret, speculate, and project the words, thoughts and emotions around us. We should enter a space of awareness of our present moment with no emotional filters, no regrets of the past or hopes for the future, with no daydreaming and no nightmares...

Ability to concentrate will give us an ability to transform a mundane situation in a very special one – just in the midst of any moment we can decide to be mindful!

LET MINDFULNESS BE YOUR EXERCISE DURING THIS WEEK. EXPERIMENT WITH MINDFULNESS, TRAIN MINDFULNESS, READ ABOUT MINDFULNESS

Mindful Being by Nuit

'A **thought weaves into another thought**, seeking the other.
The thought world has its-own Inner Life.
A rose acts upon us through its **symbolism**, through its **beauty**, through our **conscious** & **sub-conscious mind**.
Meditating we tap into the **thought form of 'rose adoration'**.

www.artof4elements.com

EXERCISE 2: LEARN HOW TO BREATH

Breath is Life.

A myth tells us that we are all given a number of breaths to 'spend' during our life-time and that it is up to us to 'use them wisely. More stressed we are, faster we breath, faster we breath, un-healthier we are and shorter we live…

We often take shallow breaths, or breath through the mouth and our diaphragm is used rarely. We often use just a fraction of our and our bodies do not get enough oxygen. With **Yoga Breathing** we exercise the proper breathing.

EXERCISE 2A: YOGA BREATHING

The **yogic breathing** teaches us to breathe through the nose, to lengthen our exhalation, increasing our physical and mental health. With **Yoga Breathing** we take the oxygen into the solar plexus. We are conscious of our breath and we take deep breaths, through the nose. This type of breathing strengthens the body and increases the supply of oxygen to the brain.

Yoga Breath is done with the following rhythm:

7 (seconds or heart beats) inhalation -1 retention – 7 exhalation – 1 retention

You could be sitting down with your back straight or lying down.

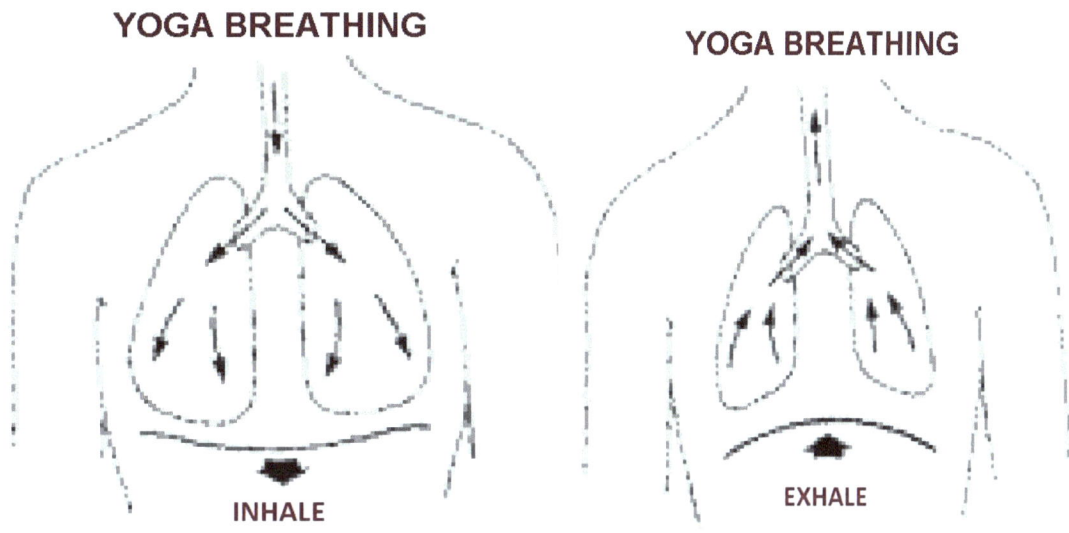

If you are sitting cross-legged, keep your shoulders relaxed. If you are a beginner, sit on a cushion, it will lift your hips and make it easier to keep the back erect. While sitting, make an effort to align your head, neck, and spine, so that the spine is perfectly straight. Head will be slightly tilted forward, and the hips will be pushed slightly forward. Place one hand on your chest and the other on your abdomen.

Breath-in pushing the air into your stomach, feeling the stomach expand. The oxygen goes into the lowest part of your lungs, then the middle, and then the top. Your chest and abdomen will expand. **Breathing slowly and deeply** brings oxygen to the lowest part of your lungs and exercises your diaphragm. During an inhalation, your diaphragm will move downwards. During an exhalation, your diaphragm moves up, compressing the lungs and pushing air out.

Practice and this will become your normal breathing, requiring no particular effort.

EXERCISE 2B   MOON VS. SUN BREATHING

Left Nostril Breathing, **Moon Breathing**, OR ACTIVATION OF IDA: is the breathing of contemplation, meditation and thinking.

Right Nostril Breathing, **Sun Breathing**, OR ACTIVATION OF PINGALA: is the breathing of action, movement, physical work.

If we wish to 'manipulate' this energy to activate our Moon breathing, when we stand we put the left leg forward, or if we are lying down, we lie on our right side, put our right hand under our head, left hand next to the stomach and left leg over the right. In this way we activate the left nostril: **Moon Breathing**.

When we stand if we put our right leg forward, or if we are lying down, we lie on our left side, put our left hand under our head, right hand next to the stomach and right leg over the left; we activate the right nostril: **Sun Breathing**

THERE ARE MANY VARIATIONS OF PRANAYAMA, BUT THIS ONE IS UNIVERSALLY EXCEPTED AS AN EXERCISE THAT HELPS THE FLOW OF PRANA (LIFE FORCE) THROUGH THE BODY.

ALTERNATE NOSTRIL BREATHING

This is an excellent breathing technique to calm and center your mind. **Sivananda** recommends it as a daily exercise that is done before **yoga** exercises or before meditation.

Do not force the breathing, keep the flow gentle and natural. Sit comfortably with your spine erect and shoulders relaxed. Your left hand is comfortably placed in your lap and your right hand will close your nostrils alternating from left to right.

Your ring finger and little finger will be closing the left nostril, and your thumb will be closing the right nostril. You will start the breath in with the right nostril and breath out with the left one. Next round of breathing will commence with the breath in with the left nostril and breath out with the right.

Then, breathe in from the right nostril and exhale from the left. And so on. Continue inhaling and exhaling from alternate nostrils.

Keep the rhythm of inhalation and exhalation of the **Yoga Breathing**: 7-1-7-1

Complete 7 rounds of this exercise every morning, just before your morning meditation. Keep your eyes closed throughout the exercise.

Concentration on breathing helps to bring the mind back to the present moment.

Practicing breathing is an ancient technique used by Yogis to harmonize the left and right hemispheres of the brain. Hindus call such breathing: Pranayama.

EXERCISE 3 IDENTIFY YOUR MENTAL FIXATIONS

Some of these mental fixations could be described as:

Mental Fixation	Emotional Consequence	Positive Alternative
I did not fully forgiven those who have hurt me, deliberate or not	I do not trust people, do not take risks, do not talk to strangers. Isolation	**I forgive**, I trust, I love
I judge or criticize others constantly. Life is never good enough.	I judge and criticize myself constantly. Cynicism and Bitterness. Anorexia, bulimia	**I will not judge or criticize**. I believe in myself. Self-confidence. Creative Flow
I gossip or talk about others	My time is constantly wasted by useless talk. I am not honest any longer	**I will not gossip.** Words are a creative force. I am careful with my words
Often I do not honestly say what I want and need	I keep everything within, get angry and explode or get sick	**I will practice honesty and truthfulness**
I never admit when I am wrong	I argue constantly, I am not careful with words and deeds	Healthy humor. We all make mistakes
I am jealous or I envy other people's success	I do not help others so others do not help me. Feel quite lonely	I rejoice with others in their success
I constantly compete	I do not work with others in harmony	Working together is **inspiring**
I blame others / circumstances for everything. I am very indecisive.	Everything is against me. I can't start or finish a project. I luck self-confidence. I am not able to make decisions.	I take risks and am able to materialize my wishes. I take **responsibility for my happiness**.

Write your own list

Start with brainstorming, noting down what your mental fixation might be:

- I do not always express my true feelings.
- I am constantly angry at my children
- I am constantly arguing with my partner
- I am quite pessimistic

Understanding our conscious and sub-conscious patterns will help us develop patterns that are empowering, so that we can express and experience our highest potential. Write the main challenges that stop you from perfecting your body, mind and that create 'noise' when you listen to your soul

Start with small steps: reduce the 'mental noise' around you (switch off TV at breakfast), improve your sleep, walk to the grosser, meditate when putting your baby to sleep.

ALCHEMY OF LOVE COURSE   MODULE 3 THINKING   EXERCISE 3 IDENTIFY MENTAL FIXATIONS

Date_____   Name_____

Mental Fixation	Emotional Consequence	Positive Alternative

EXERCISE 4 TRAIN YOUR WILL POWER

WILL POWER OUR WILL-POWER NEEDS TRAINING

Willpower needs to be trained every single day, so that it could be later used in the process of **Spiritual Development**.

You train your **Willpower** when you challenge your existing structures, when you go against your instincts, against the hunger, when you go against your sleep, when you challenge your limits whatever they are.

Write your-own list of actions for exercising Willpower during the duration of this Course. These are some of our suggestions:

- ✔ do not eat immediately when you are hungry – wait a couple of minutes, challenging your hunger
- ✔ do not sleep immediately when you are sleepy – wait a couple of minutes, challenging your sleep
- ✔ at the end of your shower, use cold water, challenging your comfort zones
- ✔ swim in cold waters
- ✔ wake up early to walk or jog
- ✔ wake up early to meditate

- ✔ run marathon
- ✔ climb Mont-Everest
- ✔ fast on water for more than 24 hours
- ✔ do not have an orgasm after 11 minutes of sex with your partner but enter into a magic of making love that might last hours
- ✔ do not get angry, even though circumstances are against you

Willpower is the basis of all Self Development Work

Train your Willpower

With the strong Willpower you will be able to invite the lady Love into your life and let Her rule from the centre of your Heart.

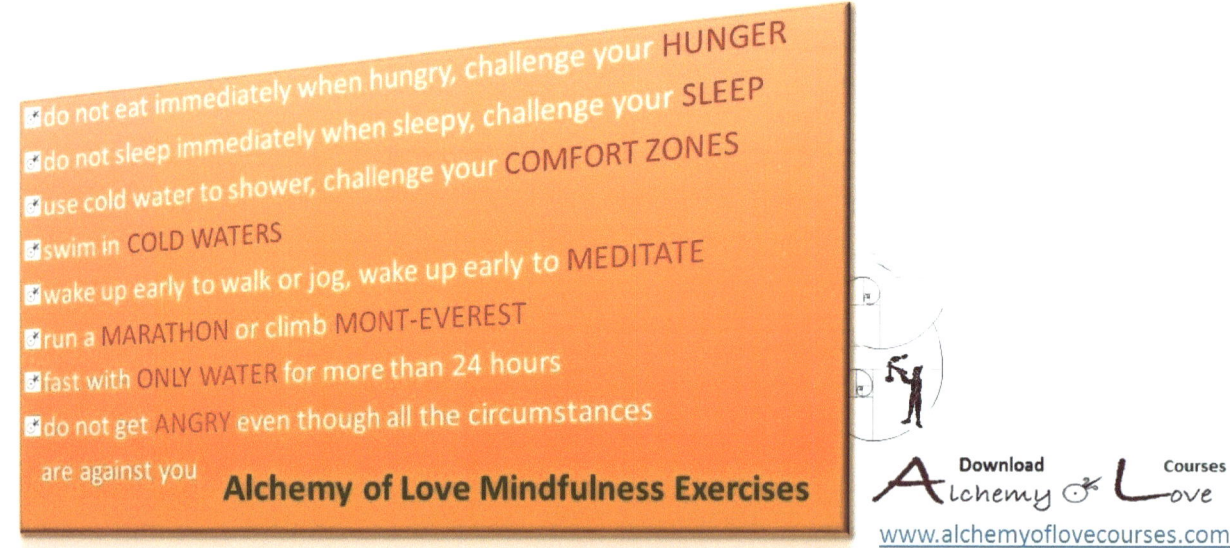

EXERCISE 5: PRACTICE CONCENTRATION AND FOCUS

FOCUS ON A DOT IN A CIRCLE

On an A4 paper draw a circle with a dot on it.

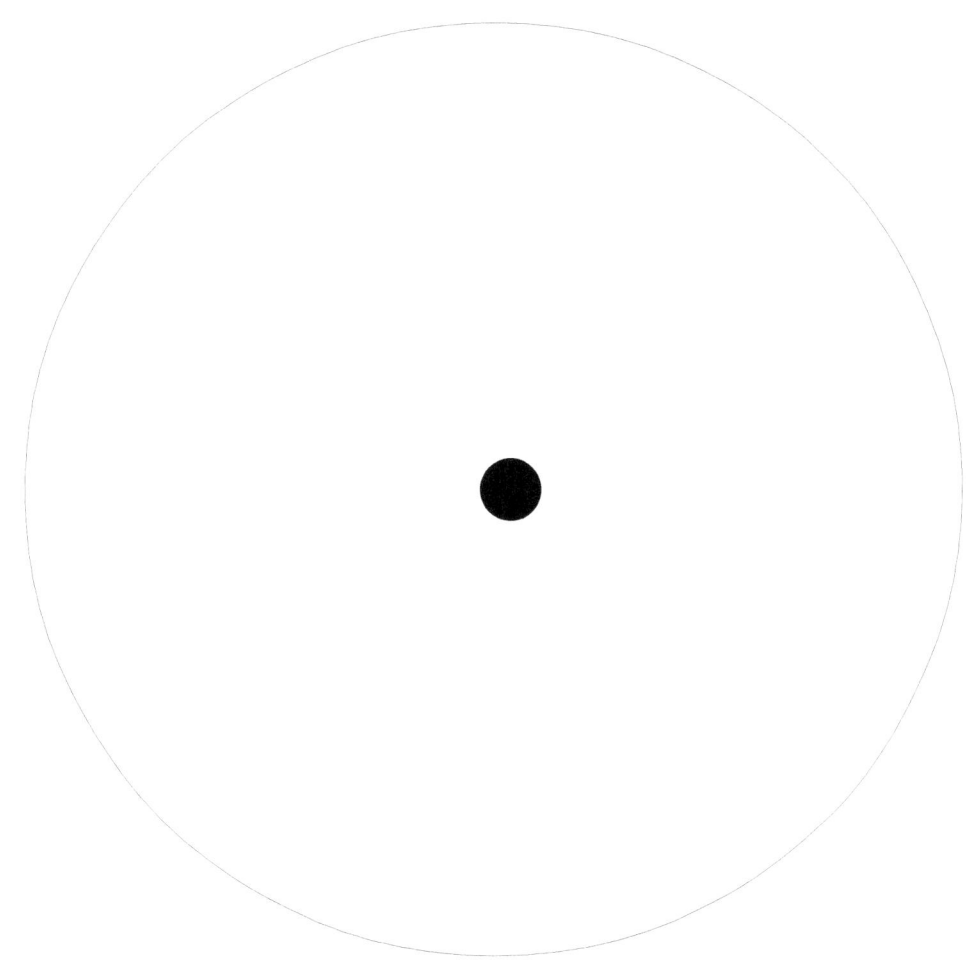

Put the drawing in front of you and observe the dot.

Imagine that the dot changes its color.

At one point of your concentration exercise, you will have a feeling that the dot has truly changed its color.

Practice this exercise standing straight with the right leg in front and later with the left leg in front opening Ida and Pingala, working with the **Moon Breathing** and the **Sun breathing**. Practice the full **abdominal yoga breathing** while you are concentrating on the black dot in front of you.

Do concentration on the dot with the **Moon Breathing for 5min** and do the concentration on the dot with the **Sun Breathing for another 5min**.

FOCUS ON A CANDLE LIGHT

Do this exercise in the evening.

Sit comfortably and lit a candle just in front of you.

Observe the flame without moving.

Fix your gaze on the flame.   Do not blink.

Stay observing the candle as long as you can.

The flame will keep this effort alive for quite a long time.

When you feel that your eyes are tiered, close them, and see the candle within your third eye.

It will be as alive as the real candle, continue focusing on its flame. Repeat the exercise once or twice. End this concentration exercise in about 10-15minutes.

IT IS GOOD TO DO THIS EXERCISE IN A GROUP. FORM A CIRCLE AND PUT A CANDLE IN THE MIDDLE OF 4-5 PEOPLE. DO NOT MOVE, DO NOT TALK, JUST OBSERVE THE FLAME.

PRACTICE YOUR CONCENTRATION...

EXERCISE 6: DRAW YOUR MANDALA

'The "squaring of the circle" is one of the many archetypal motifs which form the basic patterns of our dreams and fantasies... Indeed, it could even be called the archetype of wholeness' The mandala really is: 'Formation, Transformation, Eternal Mind's eternal recreation'. from Mandalas, C. G.Jung.

According to **Jung**, **mandala** is a **magic circle**, the symbol of the Self, formed by **archetypal forces** of the unconscious that the artist is not aware of during the creation of the work. The **symbols** and images come from the collective unconscious, these are **primordial images**, which reside in each one of us.

Mandala is a circle that represents **Wholeness**, that represents **Divine**, our relation to the **Infinite**, the world within our **body** and **mind** and the world outside. The **mandala** is used in many **spiritual traditions**.

NATIVE AMERICAN INDIANS HAVE MEDICINE WHEELS AND **SAND MANDALAS**
CIRCULAR AZTEC CALENDAR **IS IN A FORM OF A** MANDALA

The **sacred calendar of the Aztecs of Mexico** consisted of a 365-day calendar cycle and a 260-day ritual cycle. The calendar also gives a reading of the significance of each day.

Mandala Meaning in Tibet

In **Tibet**, **mandalas** have complex geometrical shapes and are often used for meditation. **Mandalas** are sometimes made of sand to emphasize the impermanence of life. When finished, the monks destroy the **mandala** sweeping it into a river, blessing the water. This action also symbolizes the **cycle of life**.

Mandalas in **Tibet**, within the tradition of **Tantric Buddhism**, are sacred geometric figures that represents the **Universe** The word '*mandala*' comes from a Sanskrit word that means 'circle'
Monks construct a **mandala** in a ritual while chanting **mantras**. In **Tibetan Buddhism**, contemplation and meditation on a **sacred image** is central to their spiritual practices and rituals, and a mandala is one of the most sacred of all images.

In Asia, the **Taoist 'yin and yang' symbol** is a mandala (circle representing Universe)

The **yin and yang** symbol consists of a circle divided into two halves - one white and the other black. Within each half is contained a smaller circle of the opposite color. The symbol represents **Tao** (Divine, Universe, God) and the primordial female (Yin) and male (Yang) energy that gives birth to all the manifested world.

Yin & Yang are co-existing together dancing their Cosmic Dance continuously transforming one into the other. One can not exist without the other, as night can not exist without day, and life can not exist without death, each contains the essence of the other.

Astrology Zodiac Circle as an Example of Mandala

The **astrology zodiac circle** is a **circle of Life** that maps all the **Universal energies** in their interplay of forces. A horoscope is a map of heavens: Sun, Moon, and the planets are in a dynamic relation to each other at a specific time, viewed from a specific place on Earth. There are 12 astrological signs with their planets and each sign and constellation of planets has its own particular energy pattern that influences people on Earth. The **astrology zodiac circle** is an attempt to understand **Universal Laws** as manifested on Earth, to comprehend **God** and its manifestation. The **astrology zodiac circle** shows the Earth at the center with the planets around it.

YOGA PRACTICE AND MANDALA

In the yoga practices **mandala** is used to support **meditation**.

Different types of **mandalas** are used to represent and worship different Gods. **Mandala** usually has an image that inspires the **Spiritual Growth**. One of the example is: **Sri Yantra or Chakra** ('holy wheel') that is a drawing of nine interlocked triangles in a circle, radiating out from the central point. It represents the creation of the **Universe** and the union of **Masculine and Feminine Divine.**

Your Mandala

Draw a circle, let the shapes and colours come from the depths of your **Soul**. **Express yourself.** Play with colours, play with shades.

Start drawing from the centre. Do not limit your imagination. Do not compete. Just draw. This is your circle. This is your **mandala**. Let it represent you.

Draw a Mandala end Remember to Enjoy the process, Remember to Play, and Love Your Work of Art!

Exercise 7: Transform Your Anger

Practice Separating from your Anger

In the moment when you are angry, when the flow of the anger energy is within your body, shaking every single cell, focus on your body, focus on your hands, focus on your breathing.

Consciously come out of your body and observe the anger, the way it activates all your sensory organs, the way it interacts with your skin, with your brain, with other feelings and thoughts.

If you are not able to focus on anything else but anger, get out of the room and walk quickly just observing your breath. **The breath should be deep and prolonged**. Then, after around 20min of fast walking, separate from anger, become an observer, there is the **Self** that observes your body and the anger.

If you are unable to go for a walk, count till 20 and back. Repeat if necessary.

Put your hand on your stomach.

If your child is angry put your hand on its shoulder. Both actions are designed with the intention to calm-down. To slow-down... Say to your anger: easy, easy... Say to your child: EASY... Easy...

'Anybody can become angry - that is easy, but to be angry with the right person and to the right degree and at the right time and for the right purpose, and in the right way - that is not within everybody's power and is not easy.' **Aristotel**

If you are angry with your child, become aware of this emotional energy of anger: what does it do to you, how do you react, how do you follow it, at which point you can stop it?

Can you move this point to an earlier time?

Can you not follow an angry thought, word, action and feel sorry afterwards?

Can you ignore the negative reaction and come back to a more rational one?

Once you have acted in anger and you feel sorry about it, tell your-self about it, tell your child about it, do not feel guilty but act differently next time.

Ask yourself: Why did I act angrily?

Sometimes we feel anger because we think that we can not do anything? We feel we will lose control and we do not like the fact that we are not in control...

FIGHT YOUR THOUGHTS ATTACKS

We all know of times when we can not concentrate and when our attention goes into 'unwanted' direction. Reading a page of a book six times, unable to 'see' it, is a good example of this 'disorder'. During these times we are visited with many '**unwanted thoughts**' and **concentration** becomes difficult.

We all experience **obsessive thinking**, when we are jealous or have just finished a relationship or fallen in love. Our ability to **concentrate** and be **mindful** is also disturbed by all the technological devices that we have: mobiles, e-mails, TV.

The quality of any life experience is about **changing of the focus**. To experience anything fully we need **mindfulness**, we need to learn how to **concentrate**.

If you have one of your 'thoughts attacks':

- ✔ go for a walk,
- ✔ go for a swim or
- ✔ go for a jog

The **physical activity** is the best for the 'obsessive thinkers'. If you an emotion 'attacks' you, you are angry with somebody, first go for a walk, jog or a swim and then try to transform this emotion into a positive one.

Put on the music and start dancing. Dance for at least 20minitues. Jump, scream, dance any way you like. When you finish dancing, sit for a moment and observe your body, and your breathing.

Sing... Singing is **healing**

Task 1 Start with your Daily Meditation

Silence is healing. **Silence is creative**. Silence is necessary. **Regular meditation** is a way to clear your mind from clutter of thoughts, a way to train **concentration** and to focus on specific themes.

Concentration

Our ## Mindful Being by Nuit

'With 70,000 thoughts a day and 95% of our activity controlled by the subconscious mind, no wonder that it feels as though we are asleep most of the time. To awake, we need to train **Self-Remembering** and **Mindfulness**.'

www.artof4elements.com

Mind is constantly active. Seeking **stillness** within the Mind that is in motion is impossible if you do not use the motion itself. When the surface of a lake is still, we will be able to see, experience, intuitively sense the ocean of our sub-conscious and to tap into the magic of super-conscious. This is impossible when the surface is agitated by waves of our thoughts, emotions, habits, fears.

In order to still our mind we will learn how to understand the body and the influence it has on our mind. The art of meditation is the art of stillness, the art of motion within no-motion, action within no-action, visualization and concentration.

Chose an object of **Beauty** that inspires you and use it as your object of **meditation** – a rose, a tree, a crystal, light...

Concentrating our mind on light, love, peace, or pure consciousness, we allow the mind to keep 'busy' while we connect with the source of power, love, peace and knowledge using powerful imagery of **positive imagination**.

Create your own **meditation**, and follow it!

Human Brain and its Magic

'I must be willing to give up what I am, in order to become what I will be.' Albert Einstein

A Human Brain is Truly Extraordinary

A healthy brain has some 200 billion neurons. Conscious mind controls our brain only 5% of the day, whereas the subconscious mind has control of our thoughts 95% of the time. A human being has 70,000 thoughts per day. The brain requires up to 20% of the body's energy despite being only 2% of the human body by weight.

Living Our Highest Potential

Somewhere, within our brain, we have a potential for higher mathematics, complex physics, art, and amazing richness of thoughts, feelings, and sensations. Somewhere, within our brain, we have a potential to understand the magic of Divine Creativity. However, we are mostly controlled by our brains, and we are yet to learn how to best use its potential.

Mindful Being by Nuit

Somewhere, within our brain, **we have a potential** for **higher mathematics**, **complex physics**, art, & amazing richness of **thoughts**, **feelings** & **sensations** Somewhere within our brain **we have a potential** to understand the **Magic** of **Creative Thinking**

Perhaps this is the task of the next phase of our evolution - utilizing our brains better, understanding the 95% of its sub-conscious functionality, becoming more creative, less bombarded by useless thoughts, more focused, and more peaceful.

Jill Bolte Taylor, PfD,, a 'human brain' scientist, who recovered from a massive left hemisphere blood clot in her book 'My Stroke of Insight' talks about her experiences during the eight years that took her to completely recover. She was unable to walk, talk, read, write or recall her life. However, she refers to this state of her being as Nirvana, a word used to describe a profound peace of mind.

RIGHT AND LEFT BRAIN

Describing the right brain, she says that the right brain is like a parallel processor. It thinks in pictures, it is non-verbal, it is non-linear, and creative. The right brain has no sense of time, it is playful, it sees humor, and it is lost in the flow. The right side of the 'human brain' is compassionate and it is associated with the heart. It is intuitive and takes us into the peacefulness of the world around us.

The left brain is like a serial processor and it is interested in the past and future. It thinks in language, and is concerned with the details. It is logical and it is the critical analytical part of our being.

The traditional educational methods, its curriculum, and the exam focus, ensure that we emphasize the development of the 'left brain' hemisphere, and with this approach the students quickly lose motivation and the interest for the science and its magic. Two fundamental assumptions of formal education are that students retain knowledge they acquired in schools, and that they can apply them in situations outside the classroom. But is this correct? How much do we really remember and how relevant our knowledge is? The likes of Albert Einstein, Leonardo da Vinci, and Mozart created their master pieces from a place of inspiration, and creativity. It is likely that they had a capability to fully utilise the virtues of both brain hemispheres.

Mindful Being   by Nuit

It was during the **Renaissance** that creativity was first seen, not as a matter of **divine inspiration**, but as a gift of a great learned man to imitate **God's ability to create**. As **Prometheus** stole the fire of the **Gods** and brought it to the mankind, humanity needed to steal the secret of '**creation**' from Gods and understand its **essence**.

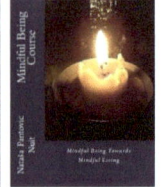

To understand children's capability to learn, educational psychology develops and applies theories of human development.

BRAIN DEVELOPMENT AND ALTERNATIVE SCHOOLING
Rudolf Steiner's model of children's development links physical, emotional, mental and moral development. In his approach he equally values rational and imaginative approach to learning, his schools teach art and dancing not only as a way of expression, but as a way of understanding and mastering cognitive thinking. An example of an alternative method of learning is a movement therapy included in the Waldorf curriculum called: Eurythmy. The word stems from Greek roots meaning *beautiful* or *harmonious rhythm. The dance is used* to awaken and strengthen the children's expression and to stimulate imagination.

Eurythmy works with mathematical forms, beginning with a straight line and curve, and proceeding to more complex geometric figures developing a child's coordination and concentration. Rods or balls are also used in exercises to develop precision in movement. Philosophically, it acknowledges a child's capacity to communicate through non-verbal gestures. **Eurythmy** is made up of discreet movements that represent various phonetic sounds**.** The feelings & thoughts have gestures that are beyond our conscious awareness. **Eurithmy** attempts to explore the variety of feelings & thoughts through the form, movement, language, rhythm, color and form. Through this art children learn the wisdom of emotional intelligence that helps their holistic growth.

Practice Divergent Thinking

Divergent thinking is essential for creativity and for what is creativity. It is the ability to see lots of possible ways to interpret a question and lots of possible answers to it.

It is a thought process used to generate creative ideas by exploring many possibilities. Instead of taking obvious steps and walking along a straight line, one looks at different aspects of the situation, creating different results.

Divergent thinking is often used as a parallel of convergent thinking that follows a particular set of logical steps to arrive at one solution. All standardised tests stipulate this type of thinking.

In their book and Beth Jarman describe a longitudinal study they conducted on 1,600 kindergarden children aged three to five. They gave them eight tests on divergent thinking and an astonishing 98 per cent of the children scored within the creative genius category.

Five years later, they re-tested the same children, now aged eight to 10 and only 32 per cent scored in the creative genius category. Five years later only 10 per cent of the children scored in this category. In tests of over 200,000 adults over 25, only two per cent scored enough to be classified as creative geniuses.

Divergent thinking tests measure an individual's ability to generate multiple approaches to solving a problem. The tests typically use simple questions such as: what are the uses for a flower pot?

An average person would have 10 to 15 answers to this question. A genius of divergent thinking would come up with a hundred possible answers, and they do this by changing the concepts of already existing thinking – can the flower pot be 10 metres wide, or can it be made of rubber, and so forth.

So what really happens with the universal **mental capability to think divergently**? What happened to those 160,000 children during their school years?

Classic Schools Educational Models and Creativity

The classic school model encourages students to adopt fixed mental models of how things work, discouraging creative thinking and problem solving. Mastering other people's mental models seems to kill an individual's ability to think divergently and wonder creatively.

We are all born with this capacity to think creatively but during the years of schooling, this capability deteriorates drastically.

Confucius: 'I hear and I forget. I see and I remember. I do and I understand.'

Brain and the Environment of Learning

The brain is a highly complex organ. The neocortex is the largest portion of the human brain. The majority of complex thought occurs in this part of the brain. Research proves that the neocortex does not function properly when people are under stress or afraid.

The classroom environment has to be safe place for students to experiment, make mistakes and take risks. The environment has to be safe to fail, revise and try again.

Right Brain Left Brain

The brain also has two distinct hemispheres, left brain versus right brain. According to the theory of left-brain or right-brain dominance, a person who is 'left-brained' is said to be more logical, and analytical, while a person who is 'right-brained' is more intuitive, thoughtful and creative.

To fully develop both hemispheres of the brain, it is important to vary thought processes so that children use both convergent and divergent thinking, both the linear, and the creative thought processes.

Divergent thinking is mostly found among people who are curious, willing to take risks, and persistent. Research shows that musicians are more likely to use both hemispheres of their brain and more likely to use divergent thinking in their thought processes.

Promoting Divergent Thinking

Activities which promote divergent thinking include:

• Encourage your child to learn how to ask questions;

• Learn how to think and be silent – allow your children to think and explore using their-own learning techniques, allow them to invent new ones, give them time and space for reflection;

• Create bridges to abstract concepts using common experiences, experiments. You should not separate learning from life; they need to find ways to use nature as a learning setting;

• Let your children write their-own stories. You can tell stories to each other, or create a story together. Allow your imagination to flow. Create your-own stage sets where you can act out scenes from books or stories that you have created.

• Work as a group: Change roles, mother should take a role of a child, father of a mother, child of a father, etc. This game can teach you many things about your child and about yourself;

• Use creative writing – writing anything that comes to mind about the given subject;

- Utilize both music and art: Draw only with colors, do not include the shape within your work, allow the colors to merge and create its-own wonder. Also, draw with your hands, the effects are amazing;

- Practice sport – working with tactics, movements and techniques, and teamwork;

- Create rich, stimulating environments using materials created by student. Changing displays regularly to provide a stimulating environment for brain development.

Einstein *'I never teach my pupils, I only attempt to provide the conditions in which they can learn.'*

PRACTICE CREATIVITY

CHALLENGING BELIEFS

Creativity refers to the invention of any new thing that has value. Someone creative has the ability to learn from traditional ideas and create new ones.

To be creative we have to choose to be different from everyone else. Learning the **skill of creativity** is about learning to challenge the existing, learning to trust one's idea, and working hard to change the world that is by default stuck in the space of 'conventional'. Creativity is an essential ingredient of one's spiritual development.

CREATIVITY AND CHALLENGING EXISTING BELIEFS
Challenging the beliefs about the world we live in and the machinery that makes it work is an essential step within the **creative process**. At all points of origination of a product, solution, or an artwork, we have a choice to reject our invention and go back to the 'norm'. At all points of the process of 'creation' we are challenged by the 'norm' and we can deny our-own mind-set, energy and feelings. Learning to access the

necessary creativity within our being and learning how to get inspired from the world around us is an essential ingredient of the creative flow.

Each of our ideas starts in the mind and it is manifested in the outside world if we have the capability to do so, or if we manage to 'sell' our invention to the people who can materialise them for us. So learning the skill of creativity, is about learning to challenge the existing, learning to trust one's idea, and working hard to change the world that is by default stuck in the space of 'conventional'.

CREATIVITY AS DIVINE INSPIRATION OR HUMAN TRAIT

It took some time for the humanity to accept 'creativity' as a possible human 'trait'. It was during the Renaissance that creativity was first seen, not as a matter of divine inspiration, but as a gift of a great learned man to imitate God's ability to create. As Prometheus stole the fire of the Gods and brought it to the mankind, humanity needed to steal the secret of 'creation' from Gods and understand its essence.

Moving from imitating and copying, to innovating and using our talents wherever we are can take time. First we need to master the particular skill: musicians have to know the rhythm, architects should know engineering concepts, artists must learn about colours and shades, writers must have the knowledge of grammar. Then we need to open our minds to the possibility of being different accepting our uniqueness.

INNOVATION & CREATIVITY

When we use our imagination to develop a new idea, the idea is inevitably structured in a predictable way, following already existing concepts. Our schools train us to think as convergent thinkers, aiming for a single, correct solution to a problem, whereas creativity demands divergent thinkers who generate multiple answers to a problem because the aim is to mediate inspiration from the unknown, to create something new.

> Dalai Lama *'Share your knowledge it is a way to achieve immortality.'*

Incubation may aid **creative problem-solving**, because it enables 'forgetting' of existing clues. We are constantly bombarded by 'solutions' so creative minds need to stay isolated from the formulas given by society, seeking for the answers in most unpredictable places

Creativity - Opening to new possibilities

A mind should not be thought to passively observe the world, but instead constantly test hypotheses to actively manipulate the environment. The expansion of mind happens when we are open to the new possibilities, when we learn how to be inspired by nature and music and by most versatile forms of art.

Our Emotional Intelligence, the expansion of our mind-set, our capability to interact with the world are all closely linked to understanding this magic of the 'divine inspiration' of creativity.

> 'YOU'RE NEVER TOO OLD, TOO WACKY, TOO WILD, TO PICK UP A BOOK AND READ TO A CHILD.' DR. SEUSS

TRANSFORMATION TOOLS ALCHEMY OF LOVE

MODULE 4 TIME / LIFE WASTERS

Mindful Being   by Nuit

How to Avoid Negative Impact of Technology?

- Stay in constant contact with **Nature**
- **Limit your time with TV, mobiles & computers**
- Spend **quality & creative time** with your loved ones: **re-invent** your time together: **sing**, **dance**, or explore learning a **new language**.

Often we do **waste time unconsciously** and we need to apply a conscious effort to record this time and activities, so that we become aware of the wasters of our life. Awareness is half of the answer. Once you are aware of where does your time go, you will do something to change this pattern.

QUESTIONNAIRE 1 YOUR TIME WASTERS

Read each sentence and rate them from 1 (really bad) to 5 (I am super happy with it). Answer to what extent you feel this statement is true.

Where does your time go?

- Wasting time watching TV
- Wasting time on Social Networking
- Wasting time on mobile / Internet
- Wasting time with games
- Wasting time gossiping, talking about others
- Wasting time sleeping
- Wasting time in laziness
- Wasting time in useless thoughts / fears / worries
- Too much of my interaction with friends / family / loved ones is shallow
- I am constantly surrounded by noise – of TV, Radio, Work Environment, etc.

WRITE THE ANSWERS OF THE PERSONALITY QUESTIONNAIRE

After you have answered your questions, meditate on answers and where the problems within your life might be. Use a colored marker to highlight areas that might need improvement. Add whatever you feel is missed out from this list. The ranking from 1 to 5 will indicate your list of priorities.

ACTION ITEM FROM THE PERSONALITY QUESTIONNAIRE

Study each answer that you are not happy with and determine what precise action you would like to do to change your state of body, mind, emotions.

Write down the areas that need improvement. Compare them with the areas that need to be protected from the Circle of Activities of Your Ideal Life. Be specific...

ALCHEMY OF LOVE COURSE MODULE 4 TIME WASTERS OBSERVATION EXERCISE 1

Date_____   Name_____

Your Time Wasters	Day 1	Day 2	Day 3	Day 4	Quality (1-5)	Quantity (1-5)
TV						
Games						
Social Networking Sites (Facebook, etc)						
Computer						
Mobile						
Messaging						
eMail						

1 unit = 1 hour of time spent

Your Notes:

Exercise 1: Master Your Daily Habits

Emails, ads, text messages, phone calls, and chatting keep us **BUSY** but they overload our minds and over-complicate our schedules. No wonder we're stressed and out of balance! A typical American receives and processes over 197 messages - emails, ads, text messages, phone calls every day.

SWITCH OFF YOUR MOBILE DURING THIS WEEKEND!
- Yes, it is possible to live without a mobile during the weekend, try the old way of phoning people, it is quite interesting

SWITCH OFF YOUR COMPUTER DURING THIS WEEKEND

SWITCH OFF YOUR TV / RADIO DURING THIS WEEKEND

DO NOT READ ANYTHING DURING THIS WEEKEND

TAKE OFF YOUR WRIST-WATCH

DO NOT USE YOUR CAR DURING THIS WEEKEND

Spend time with your loved ones (not in a hotel, travelling, busy with different sets of impulses, but at home, just using different tools)

Stay just with yourself, without any technology, and observe the power of Synchronicity that exist within our lives, that we can experience when we are not overloaded with 197 messages sent from friends and strangers of all sort. The Universe will reward your experiment, will reward you for taking risks and you will be training your sense of inner perception.

A Few Ideas to keep your life inspired while you switched off all the technology:

- Meditate
- Play an instrument (re-discover your guitar or just start playing jembe)
- Play with your kids or your sister's kids, Play with your pets
- If you are a dad – cook with your kids; if you are a mum – go and play football with them
- Dance
- Talk to strangers
- Walk, exercise, spend time in Nature, Laugh

Human Brain and Technology

Inspired or Lost within Technology Matrix

We live surrounded by an increasingly complex matrix of impulses allowing strangers of all sorts (TV, media, Internet) interfere in our mental, emotional and spiritual development. Understanding this intricate network and how does the human brain interacts with it is becoming our door to happiness and health.

The self or the personality is a bundle of socially influenced traits that emerges and gets formed gradually. We are shaped by our parents and neighbors, by our religion, the media, by various marketing agendas of major corporations, by our state's politics, by the way we behave or misbehave towards our-own body, our mind, environment, animals and plants, and our planet Earth. So, what would we need to do to understand the importance of a healthy body, to manage our emotions and nurture love for our friends and family, to become aware of how we can make a positive impact on our society or the environment, or discover the purpose of life and ways to be happy?

Human Brain and TV

A great deal is known about our behavior and TV, and our emotions and computer games, because there have been thousands of studies on these subjects. The researchers have all asked the same question - whether there is a link between exposure to violence (on TV or within a game) and violent behavior. Most of the studies answered: 'yes – the link is there'. According to the AAP (American Academy of Pediatrics), 'Extensive research evidence indicates that media violence can contribute to aggressive behaviour, desensitization to violence, nightmares, and fear of being harmed.' An average American child will see 200,000 violent acts and 16,000 murders on TV by age 18...

None of us wants to see our children or our loved ones depressed, obese, in front of computers or TV screens at all times, having behavioral problems, being sick, or experiencing attention deficit hyperactivity disorder. However, the rhythm of our lives and our day-to-day habits might have an adverse effect on our mental health.

Human Brain and Mobiles

Human brain does some very sophisticated ordering of its incoming nerve impulses. Any information that we are exposed to becomes knowledge when it is translated and related to the personal experience, to the feelings, or desires. When we look at an image, our perception of an image is colored by our emotions. There is a reciprocal relationship between the area of the brain responsible for logical thinking and the area that is the seat of our emotion. Within the world of technology, numbers, letters, adverts, '**human brain**' has to constantly perform little miracles of de-coding, detachment, de-stress, and de-tox to keep us sane and free of diseases. As we grow older, and stronger in our wish to stay healthy and happy, our need for creativity grows, we constantly luck time to be physically active, to read and reflect, to play, and amongst all, we luck the quality time with our friends and family. The interaction with the NET, with the TV, with the computer has replaced the interaction with nature that in its magic way nurtures our cognitive, emotional, physical and psychological well-being.

A group of friends socializing will have a number of mobiles handy on the table, easily within reach for checking e-mails, showing off photos, or answering a call. This invisible 'best friend' and inseparable 'commodity' could prove to be our 'worst enemy'...

A recent study by Andrew Przybylski and Netta Weinstein of the University of Essex observed couples of strangers discussing a meaningful topic for 10 minutes with or without a cell phone nearby. The pairs who tried to 'connect' in the presence of a cell phone repeatedly reported **lower relationship quality** and less closeness with the assigned 'chatting' partner. The studies suggest that because of the many 'entertainment' options phones give us they distort our ability to connect with the people right next to us.

"The presence of a mobile phone may orient individuals to thinking of other people and events outside their immediate social context. In doing so, they divert attention away from a presently occurring interpersonal experience to focus on a multitude of other concerns and interests." said the lead researcher Andrew Przybylski.

A study for the Journal of Behavioural Addictions in the US analysed the data from 191 business students from two universities and revealed that students send on average 110 texts a day, or approximately 3,200 messages a month and check their phones 60 times in a typical day. Nomophobia is the term for people who experience anxiety when they have no access to their mobiles.

HUMAN BRAIN AND INSPIRATION

An electronic 'connection' interferes with our human relationships. Saying 'I love you' and texting 'I love you' could have completely different connotations based on body language. Discounting the value of nonverbal cues leads to an amazing amount of mis-understandings.

Text messages are used in our romantic and sexual correspondence. A wonderful romantic love letter became obscure. Texting is quick, easy, and convenient and notwithstanding its 160 characters limitation, some people use it to exchange important information with their romantic partner. Messages are often misinterpreted, often edited, forwarded, or written by somebody else. The stress caused by the response expectation is unique for this type of communication. A lack of response to a text message from a potential romantic partner is often deciphered as a form of rejection.

So, how to help our minds stay inspired and enthusiastic and our relationships stay healthy?

- Limit your time with TV, mobiles and computers;

- If you are spending the time with people you really care about, you might want to re-consider the habit of reaching for your phone to reply to a text message or checking your e-mail.

- Spend quality time with your loved ones, re-invent your time together: sing, dance, do art together, or explore learning a new language;

- Experiment, challenge the existent, and stay curious;

- Stay in constant contact with nature.

MODULE 5 FEELINGS

Mindfulness & Conscious Living

We will help you examine your world of feelings and emotions.

OBSERVE YOUR FEELINGS

We are capable of such an amazing range of Feelings. Feelings make us Human. The Emotional Intelligence is a skill and an art form. Do you understand your feelings? Do you let your feelings inspire you or rule and ruin your life? Do you connect to your-own Feelings? Are the Feelings yours or do they belong to the rest of the Humankind? Out of the shadow of a Human Soul, out of Conscious and Unconscious Behavior. They can be tamed yet not controlled, they can become our obsession or our Creative Force.

Meditate upon the following words and answer to what extent do you feel this way right now.

- Inspired
- Creative
- Curious
- Loving
- Excited
- Strong
- Enthusiastic
- Full of energy & action

ALCHEMY OF LOVE COURSE   MODULE 5 FEELINGS   QUESTIONNAIRE 1 TODAY I FEEL

Date_____   Name_____

Describe Your Feeling	Day 1	Day 2	Day 3	Day 4	Quality (1-5)	Quantity (1-5)
Inspired						
Creative						
Curious and full of wonder						
Full of Love						
Excited						
Mentally Strong						
Enthusiastic						
Full of energy & action						

WRITE THE ANSWERS OF THE PERSONALITY QUESTIONNAIRE

Once you perhaps sensed or identified your problems, use the words – I feel:

- Confused
- Lonely
- Guilty
- Stressed-out
- Scared and Irritable
- Lazy and All the Time without Energy
- Too Nervous
- Negative or Skeptic

This is a Journey. Your Feelings are your Guide, your Advisers, your Primary contact with Your Soul. Let's Respect them. Let's Understand them. Let's Work with them.

Have a virtue per month that you are focusing on. Chose to:

- exercise openness,
- exercise truthfulness,
- exercise courage.

Art of 4 Elements by Nuit

EXERCISE 1: EXERCISE AWARENESS

The quality of life is in proportion of our **capacity to get delighted**.

The capacity for delight is within our capacity to pay attention to things around us. So, during this week pay attention to birds singing, to clouds formations, to flowers that greet you, to kids laughing, to a beautiful person that has just passed by.

Be aware of interconnectedness of all living beings and be alert for the presence of **Divine in All**.

> 'IF YOU REALISE YOUR TRUE SELF, YOU WILL NOT NEED SUFFERING, YOU WILL UNDERSTAND WHAT A WASTE OF TIME SUFFERING IS, WHEN CONSCIOUSNESS CAN BECOME YOUR CHOICE. ON THE OPPOSITE SIDE OF SUFFERING YOU FIND LOVE. SO, TO STOP LONGING FOR THE STATES OF SUFFERING, WE NEED TO ACTUALLY TRAIN OURSELVES IN LOVING! WE NEED TO LEARN TO BREATH LOVE, SPEAK LOVE AND BE LOVE EVERY SINGLE MOMENT OF OUR LIVES. LOVE CONTROLLED BY WILL.'

Alchemy of Love

Nataša Pantović **Nuit**

from Spiritual Novel **A-Ma**

www.artof4elements.com

EXERCISE 2: YOUR SOUL'S DIARY

This is a wonderful **tool** that came to me when I needed it the most, when my mind was confused, my emotional body ruptured, my energy flow low. I kept using it all throughout my life with the greatest benefits. Trust its efficiency, it will surprise you.

Buy yourself a most beautiful Diary. Give your Soul this Gift. Let it be there for you to Feel it, Notice it, Remember it. Let IT be Yours. Your Soul's Diary or **Stream of consciousness writing** is done early in the morning, and it is about recording your thoughts, feelings, and your day-dreaming. The writing is done without any judgment, without conclusions, without any particular intention.

You should just follow your **Stream of Consciousness**. Do not interfere – write!

This writing becomes the **Diary of your Soul**.

The various revealing patterns will enfold, sometimes confusing, sometimes worrying, when you start exploring the depth of your Soul's secrets. Do not Judge. Do not Guide. Do not Stop. Do not Read. Just write.

Writing the **Diary of your Soul** is healing.

Your writings should not be organized into any sort of topics. You should allow yourself to write nonsense, to write rubbish, to write gibberish, to draw, to express in any way what is within you.

If you get stuck start with recalling your dreams that night and let your **Soul** do the rest of the talking.

Try not to read your Diary just after you have written it. Allow it to sit for a week, without any review, or judgment. This will encourage your **Soul** to go deeper into **Truthfulness** and your writings will become more inspired. Follow the flow of whatever comes along and do it every morning!

NOBODY EXCEPT YOU WILL READ YOUR DIALOG WITH YOUR SOUL

EXERCISE 3: PRACTICE VIRTUES

For a week at a time, cultivate a single **noble quality**: love, honesty, clarity, tolerance, non-violence, or positive thinking. **Read about this quality**, **meditate** on this quality, **do art works related to this quality**, talk to people about it, work with it, let IT becomes you.

If you are **practicing virtues** – you will observe your actions in thoughts, words and deeds.

Thoughts are very potent. Do not ignore them. If you think negative of somebody, that thought will poison you and you will turn it against yourself, soon you will be thinking negative thoughts about yourself. That's the law of nature.

But, most of all: **Practice Truthfulness**

> 'A child has a deep longing to discover that the **World is based on Truth.** Respect that longing. In our attempt to help children **grow into Inspired Adults,** we wish them to carry the **Youthfulness of their Souls,** and the **Wonders of Childhood into their old age.'**   **Conscious Parenting** by Nuit

Exercise 3A: Practice Truthfulness

Be truthful. With the truth you will get other virtues. Don't tell lies. The lies stick onto you, they become a habit and the mind starts uttering them before you are aware of consequence of lying.

Our society is based around little lies that are served to children from very early on. We lie about Santa Claus, we lie about tooth fairies, we lie about little 'do's and 'don't-s, 'can' or can not-s because lying seems easier. However our little ones quickly find out what is the truth and are quick to adopt lying as a norm within their lives. It is easier in long term to practice truthfulness and to have the truth instead of a lie as a normal behavior.

What does it mean – Practice Virtue?

Exercise 3B: Practice Compassion

Practice Compassion

Find an example of the best follower of this virtue.

For example, **Dalai Lama is embodiment of Compassion**.

If you are practicing **Compassion**, read his work about **Compassion**, introduce **Compassion** in your every-days life, put a photo of Dalai Lama on your desk, so that it reminds you about his work and the quality of **Compassion**.

Write about **Compassion**. Watch films that inspire **Compassion**

Meditate about **Compassion**. **Feel the Compassion** within your heart.

Wake up with a Compassionate thought. Go to sleep with **Compassion** within your heart.

Talk to people about **Compassion. Live Compassion!**

Practice Compassion!

EXERCISE 3C: PRACTICE ASSERTIVENESS

Meditate about Assertiveness. Assertiveness has two aspects – the one of determination and the one of awareness of wishes, thoughts, feelings and behavior patterns.

Answer the following questions and see how relevant this subject is to your life:

- When your opinion is different from the opinion of the person you respect, are you capable to express your opinion?
- Are you happy to accept positive criticism and suggestions that go with it?
- Do you know how to ask for help when you need one?
- Do you believe in your own judgment?
- If somebody else has a better solution than you, do you accept it?
- Do you express your thoughts, opinions and feelings honestly, openly and truthfully?
- Do you know how to find solutions that are compromising?

You can make an assertiveness statement that relates to your goals in life. **For example:**

> 'I am determined to live my highest potential at all times of my life. I am determined to stay awake and aware of my wishes, thoughts and feelings. My will power will direct my action towards my true wishes, thoughts and feelings.'

_____
_____
_____

Think about the quality of assertiveness in relation to your life. When is it that you do not live this quality in the right way? **For example**:

> 'If I am worried about other people's thoughts and feelings, I do not express myself properly. I often find myself not being assertive within the work environment with my colleagues.'

> 'Often I act in a way that the most people will act and I have a problem to determine which one of our many 'I's represents my true feelings, thoughts and wishes.'

_____
_____

When do I exercise assertiveness in the best possible way?

> 'When surrounded by strangers, when faced with the unknown, I stay determined in my wish to live my highest potential. I do not become scared or lost in confusion but stay determined to act the way I believe it is the best.'

_____
_____
_____
_____

I can express assertiveness in the best way when:

- I honor my Self
- I know what I want
- When I am aware of the situation, surroundings and causes and effects. Awareness guides me through this matrix of karmic influences, subconscious chains, and invisible lies to the understanding of True Self.

_____
_____
_____
_____

What are the negative aspects of Assertiveness? **For example**:

> 'I have a difficulty to distinguish assertiveness from aggression. I find assertiveness often becomes **aggressive and borders with selfishness**. I wish to stay assertive about my wishes and thoughts without hurting others and without being aggressive.'

_____
_____
_____
_____

MODULE 6 CORE BELIEFS

Free Your Conscious & Sub-conscious Mind

Free Mind

Journey to Happiness

Creative Flow

Divine Inspiration

Mindfulness Training

Your enemy within are your core negative beliefs. Negative beliefs hide from the consciousness and they get exposed by the magic of mindfulness and awareness. **Mindfulness and Awareness is half of the battle won.**

Understanding Core Beliefs

Core beliefs are at the very essence of how we **perceive ourselves**, and the world around us. Core beliefs are rigid, hard and inflexible. Core beliefs are sentences and words that are repeated so many times that they became our truth. **Core beliefs** identify who we are, what we are allowed to do or be, and how do we behave and react to people, experiences and life.

Everywhere we turn, someone will tell us how to think, how to look, what to feel, what to say, how to live. The news will give us a message of a dangerous world, the magazines will shape our sense of beauty, TV will teach us that money is happiness and beauty is in the youth, and our consumer society will shape our needs and wants. We are constantly bombarded by the messages of what to believe in, how to think, or what to do.

Our core beliefs are at the root of our unhappiness, our low self-esteem, our destiny.

One of the strongest **existing beliefs** we all have is that we will be happy if other people like us.

For other people to like us we try our best to be 'liked' complying with the current 'norm' whatever the 'norm' is. This leads to a major flow of **EXPECTATIONS and DISHONESTY** about ones True feelings and thoughts.

The society has set a norm of **Beauty as a Value**. Youth is Beautiful. To comply with this 'norm' we undertake plastic surgeries, we diet to exhaustion, we develop bulimia or anorexia, but nothing truly helps because at one point or another we DO GET OLD.

To be truthful to ones feelings, you need to distinguish which of the feelings / thoughts are actually yours and which are the product of mass marketing and socially established norms.

My little daughter tells me that her favorite color is PINK. Do I believe her or is it so, because a crazy media machine pushes PINK as girls' color. My mum, fairy-tales, and society tell me that the **happiness** is within the institution of Marriage. No wonder all hell breaks loose when we discover that we are married and not as yet happy. It is important that we challenge our beliefs and that we develop alternative, balanced beliefs.

If we change our beliefs, we can hope to change our reality

QUESTIONNAIRE 1 MY CORE BELIEFS

This questionnaire contains a number of statements that describe core beliefs, and they will help you identify Beliefs that Guide Your Life.

Read each item and rate them from 1 (lowest) to 5 (highest). Answer to what extent you feel this way right now, that is, at the present moment.

Successful	Unsuccessful
Responsible	Irresponsible
Open	Closed
Happy	Unhappy
Loved	Not Loved
Honest	Dishonest
Relaxed	Tense
Consistent	Inconsistent
Hard working	Lazy
Entertaining	Boring
Determined	Undetermined
Courageous	Fearful

WRITE THE ANSWERS OF THE PERSONALITY QUESTIONNAIRE

ALCHEMY OF LOVE COURSE   MODULE 6 CORE BELIEFS   QUESTIONNAIRE 1

Date_____   Name_____

	My Core Belief		1	2	3	4	5
1	Successful	Unsuccessful					
2	Responsible	Irresponsible					
3	Open	Closed					
4	Happy	Unhappy					
5	Loved	Not Loved					
6	Honest	Dishonest					
7	Relaxed	Tense					
8	Consistent	Inconsistent					
9	Hard working	Lazy					
10	Entertaining	Boring					
11	Determined	Undetermined					
12	Courageous	Fearful					

My List of Priorities:

Items Marked as 1, 2 and 3 are:

My Core Belief	1	2	3

After you have answered your questions, **meditate** on answers and where the problems within your life might be.

Use a colored marker to highlight areas that might need improvement. Add whatever you feel is missed out from this list. The ranking from 1 to 5 will indicate your list of priorities.

ACTION ITEM FROM THE PERSONALITY QUESTIONNAIRE

Analyze your list of priorities. Listen to your internal dialogue for:

- 'I can't…',
- 'I'm afraid…',
- 'I am not well equipped'
- 'Circumstances are not just right – maybe not just now…'

Become conscious of thoughts that slow down your inspiration, your creativity, your spiritual progress. Focusing on negative qualities is letting fear and habits ruin your chances for happier and healthier life. Diagnose your malady and find its proper cure.

Identify limiting belief   Identify more useful belief

Apart from the virtues that we have already mentioned, the positive beliefs that you can work with are.

- CRITICAL THINKING and ANALYTICAL REASONING

- OPEN-MINDEDNESS and FLEXIBILITY

- LOVE for people around you

- LOVE for plants and animals

- LOVE of learning

- TOLERANCE for DIFFERENT PERSPECTIVES

- PERSEVERANCE and PERSISTENCE,

- TRUTHFULNESS and HONESTY

- ENTHUSIASM and OPTIMISM

- KINDNESS and GENEROSITY

- SELF-LESS SERVICE

- MODESTY and HUMILITY

- SELF-CONTROL and SELF-RESTRICTION

- GRATITUDE and THANKFULNESS

- PLAYFULNESS and HUMOR

You can easily find the positive intention of any negative belief – write your own!

Exercise 1 What are your LIMITING BELIEFS
Your Core Beliefs will manifest in life as an inability to do some concrete things like:

Limiting Belief	Positive Alternative
I don't like myself and nobody likes me!	I am on a self-development journey and I do my best to live my highest potential. I am surrounded by love.
I am a creative person that welcomes new ideas and challenges stuck in a box of routine and boredom	I will create a set of circumstances, surround myself with friends and stay within a surrounding that inspires me and keeps me mentally and emotionally satisfied
Whatever I do, I fail…	I do not consider a failure as good or bad. I try to learn from it and I continue entering the challenges, doing the best I can.
I am too busy for my family and for love	I am never busy to love. Love connects me with my life-flow and keeps me creative and satisfied.
My mistakes worry me and discourage me.	I learn from my mistakes. Go and do work in Africa to put yourself into perspective of how some people live and work
I believe that we all need to struggle and suffer to grow	I learn to train love, peacefulness, conscious and mindful being. I am in love with Life.
I do not like my job or the repetitive nature of my job	I will change my job
Worry and pettiness deplete me from energy and give me an emotional fatigue	I refuse to let worry and pettiness in my life. There is so much beauty around me so I will not waste my time!
I am just not able to finalize any projects because of my fear of failure	I feel confident that as my knowledge increases, my new projects will succeed.

Now, write down what are the Beliefs you would like to adopt

CHANGE THE LIST OF YOUR NEGATIVE CORE BELIEFS INTO A LIST OF POSITIVE INTENTIONS
You are who you believe you are. Your reality is shaped by these major beliefs

Add the part with negative beliefs that are transformed into positive beliefs.

ALCHEMY OF LOVE COURSE   MODULE 6 CORE BELIEF   EXERCISE 1 IDENTIFY CORE BELIEFS

Date_____   Name_____

Limiting Belief	Emotianal Consequence	Positive Alternative

Mindful Being   by **Nuit**

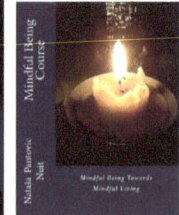

Our enemy within are our Core Negative Beliefs.
Negative beliefs hide from the Consciousness and they get exposed by the Magic of **Mindfulness** and **Awareness**.
Explore Your **Core Beliefs, Challenge Existing,** Train **Mindfulness**, Understand **Beauty**, Work with Emptiness, **Meditate**

EXERCISE 2 DRAW A FLOWER OF BELIEFS

Draw a flower with 4 petals. In the centre is 'I'. Write down your qualities or virtues that inspire you most.

1st petal

Write people that inspire you and their qualities. Write a name of a philosopher, scientist, saint that inspire you for whatever reason. Write one word next to each name.

2nd petal

Write skills that you wish to have and activities that might inspire you (music, art, and writing, sport)

3rd petal

Write 2 personal goals for this year that you wish to fulfill. It is recommended that these goals are related to the skills and qualities you wish to develop.

4TH petal

Write down something that you have achieved in your life and that makes you very proud. Do not forget to feel grateful for the successes that you already had within your life. Appreciate them and give them time and space in your life.

Exercise 3 My Name

Each one of the family members should write down his or her name vertically on a piece of paper and list a number of qualities that have the same first letter as letters of the name. Draw what this quality means to you...

What is its color, shape, what is the person or animal that represents it?

This can become a little game where you all discuss the qualities and when were these qualities most visible within your relationship.

A Attractive

N Nice

A Aware

An Alphabet drawing used in Steiner Schools

Exercise 4 Challenge Existing Beliefs

One of the strongest **existing beliefs** we all have is that we will be happy if other people like us. For other people to like us we try our best to be 'liked' complying with the current 'norm' whatever the 'norm' is. This leads to a major flow of **EXPECTATIONS and DISHONESTY** about ones True feelings and thoughts.

The society has set a norm of **Beauty as a Value**. Youth is Beautiful. To comply with this 'norm' we undertake plastic surgeries, we diet to exhaustion, we develop bulimia or anorexia, but nothing truly helps because at one point or another we DO GET OLD.

To be truthful to ones feelings, you need to distinguish which of the feelings / thoughts are actually yours and which are the product of mass marketing and socially established norms.

My girl tells me that her favorite color is PINK. Do I believe her? Or is it so, because a crazy media machine of our time pushes PINK as girls' color.

If your child tells you that someone is ugly, ask him/her to explain what exactly is ugly, what the ugliness is, tell him that you do not quite understand and leave the child with the question.

My mum, fairy-tales, and society tell me that the **happiness** is within the institution of Marriage. No wonder all hell breaks loose when we discover that we are married and not as yet happy.

Who am I?

What am I?

What makes me happy?

What are the whispers of my Soul?

How to listen to them?

To be able to answer these questions, first and foremost we need to challenge our relationship with the 'norm'.

Chose any of the following exercises to 'break' the chains of society that are tightly woven around your neck:

- Go walking backwards
- Stop next to the street music player and start dancing and singing with him
- Go to a nudist beach
- If you are a man – put on nail-polish on one of your fingers
- Do not wear under-pants
- Stop to talk with strangers
- If in a crowded street, just stop and observe the crowd moving next to you
- If in an argument, choose a point of view that is not yours and argue it as though it is yours
- If you never go by train, try going by a train; if you never go by bus, go by bus
- Invent your-own exercise that challenge your relationship with the 'norm'

Have lots of FUN!

Tasks:

- T1 Meditate in the morning – learn to get in touch with silence within yourself
- T2 Set your clock ½ hour earlier and write a page of stream-of-consciousness writing. From today, do it every day for the next 6 weeks
- T3 Read your Soul's Diary. Reading the words that you have written will give you a shift in perspective and you might be able to identify some of your core beliefs. Reading what you wrote, and observing the words you speak are practices of self awareness.

Our Core Beliefs Article: Clichés and myths of Sexual attractiveness

So an ideal female would be in her 20s with a childish looking face, with big breasts, small nose, big lips and with 'happiness' written all over her 'blonde Barbie' personality, and an ideal man would be in his 40s, proud, sexy, non-smiling, and wealthy of-course, with his Prince Charles personality.

People often follow clichés and myths about what makes someone sexy leaving the Industry's Big Brothers an amazing playing field to develop a complex set of marketing rules and launch 100s of products that exploit and manipulate the subconscious traits that govern the everlasting game of sexual attraction.

Our sensitivity to beauty seems to be encoded within our make-up and shaped by our evolution. We love to look at facial symmetry, smooth skin, long shiny hair, and sexy bodies because they all convey the same message – this person is healthy and strong, it has more robust genes hence our offspring will survive. The Greeks believed that there are three ingredients to beauty: symmetry, proportion, and harmony. Plato wrote of so-called 'golden proportions' that is found as beautiful in nature, humans and works of art, in both music and painting. He talks about the 'golden ratio' of 1:1.618 that is found in spirals, leafs, and growing patterns in Nature... The ration between the width of the mouth and the width of the nose fits this ratio. The symmetry between the left and right sides of the face is also very important to a human perception of attractiveness.

The Western beauty gurus have their-own stereotypes preferring females with a small jaw, smaller nose, large eyes, longer and more slender legs, curved hips and larger breasts, spiralling the growth of surgical interventions that enhance these parts of the body.

In 2011, chasing their ideal of beauty Americans had nearly 14 millions cosmetic procedures including collagen and botox injections, breast implants, buttock lifts and nose jobs. Breast enhancement is still on the top of the list of surgical procedures amounting to 307,180 breasts implants in 2011. If you multiply this number by 10 – a number of years of this 'false tits' frenzy - you will come to an approximate but still amazing number of 30 million women who had breast implants in the US.

Physical traits often associated with masculinity are height, firm mussels, broader shoulders, and smaller hip-to-waist ratios. Plastic surgery statistics in the UK tell us that a record number of male 'tummy tuck' operations were done in 2011, a demand that outshines even the women's breast enlargements.

The 'ideal' face is often described as 'baby' face that sends messages to our eternal Self searching for innocence, virginity, and purity. In Japan 'child-like' preference in female faces is further manipulated by sex shops offering used panties for sale with the odour of schoolgirls' body. In the Land of Rising Sun, this fascination with schoolgirls' virginity is also used by dozen of magazines that are devoted to bura-sera photographs, pictures that feature girls in school uniforms holding up their skirts to display their panties.

That brings us to the **scent as an ingredient to the sexual attractiveness**. Let me smell your pheromones (scented sex hormones) and I will tell you what I think about you... Smelling one another hands or faces is a nearly universal human behaviour. Pheromones were first defined in 1959 as chemicals animals excrete to attract their mates. The evolutionary bouquet offer a wide range of proofs for this behaviour: a male dog pursuing the scent of a female; monkeys that rub the urine on their feet to attract mates, etc. Laboratory researchers have found many relations between the scents and our moods. Such findings have led to the development of aromatherapy:

- A trace of lemon increases people's awareness of their health;
- Lavender contributes to a pleasant mood;
- Sandal wood relaxes the mind and de-stresses the body

Interesting facts about perfumes on the Net tell us that in Victorian England, a nice-smelling young lady could sell handkerchiefs scented with their body odor!

Many perfume makers would love to see their scent as a magic potion increasing hugging, kissing and sexual attractiveness. However, women who believe that the use of 'sexy' perfumes will attract men, may be misguided. Researches show that a women's sensitivity to musk, an ingredient used in perfumes, is 1000 times greater than men's.

A study conducted by the Smell and Taste Research Foundation in Chicago discovered that a variety of odors can increase penile blood-flow. These odours included pumpkin pie, liquorice, doughnuts and lavender, and oriental spices.

> What people find attractive has been shaped by centuries of evolutionary and cultural forces. Some evolutionary theories suggest that females are attracted to stern, silent and dominant males because they convey that they are strong and valuable hence able to provide for their offspring. Some of them even link smiling with a lack of dominance, an emotion best left to females. A fact that most men marry younger women led to researches proving that men prefer younger women and women prefer older, wealthier men.

Transformation Tools Alchemy of Love

Module 7 Relationships

Train Unconditional Love ➡ Conscious Relationships

This module is designed to help you examine your relationships, your ability to love and tune into your-own and other people's wants and needs.

QUESTIONNAIRE 1 RELATIONSHIP QUESTIONNAIRE

Mark each statement from 1(strongly disagree) to 5 (fully agree) by indicating how much you agree or disagree with it.

- I am in tune with my wants and needs

- I love my-Self

- I feel love and compassion for my parents and I often tell them that I love them

- I get along well with my siblings – we share, we laugh, we play together

- I get along well with my co-workers and manager/staff.

- I have a circle of friends/family who love and appreciate me for who I am

- I listen to my friends when they are upset

- My partner empowers me, he believes in me, and supports what I do.

- I usually discuss my problems and concerns with my friends / partner.

- I spend enough time with friends in good quality exchange

Alchemy of Love Course   Module 7 Relationships   Questionnaire 1

Date_____   Name_____

My Relationships	1	2	3	4	5
I am in tune with my wants and needs and I love my-Self					
I feel love and compassion for my parents and I often tell them that I love them					
I get along well with my siblings – we share, we laugh, we play together					
I get along well with my co-workers and manager/staff.					
I have a circle of friends/family who love and appreciate me for who I am					
My partner empowers me, he believes in me, and supports what I do.					
I spend enough time with friends in good quality exchange					

My List of Priorities: Items Marked as 1, 2 and 3 are:

My Relationships	1	2	3

WRITE ANSWERS TO THE PERSONALITY QUESTIONNAIRE

ACTION ITEM FROM THE PERSONALITY QUESTIONNAIRE

Study each answer that you are not happy with and determine what precise action you would like to do to change your state of body, mind, emotions.

Write down the areas that need improvement. Be specific...

- My partner makes me doubt myself.
- I find that my partner don't want to get as close as I would like.
- I prefer not to show my friends how I feel deep down.
- It's easy for me to be affectionate and loving.
- I Run after other people in the quest for affection
- I have lack of friends
- My relationship with my parents destroy my self-confidence and I feel a lack of appreciation
- I am not able to attract the type of people I want into my life
- I try to impress others
- I don't have enough time off to socialize / improve my relationships
- I get too easily irritated with my parents
- I get too easily irritated with my partner
- I get too easily irritated with my kids
- My sister / brother and I argue all the time
- I constantly feel pressure at my work.
- My boss is too critical
- My kid's habits get on my nerves

After you have identified your problem areas, find the ways to improve the most important relationships within your life.

Write a list of actions.

For Example:

- Make a point not to argue with your parents next time you see them – let this be a conscious exercise

- Let your partner know that s/he is too critical and that her/his criticism is too destructive for you

- When you criticize someone make sure that your criticism is constructive

- Socialize with people that have similar interests to you and **deepen your friendships**

- Make a point to stop judging and blaming yourself. Change what you need to change but do not keep on worrying about your attitudes

Mindful Being   by Nuit

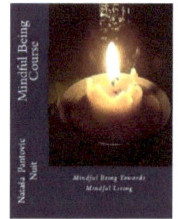

We train ourselves all through our life **to waste energy** following **our inner narratives**. We are often **unconsciously driven** by our fears, worries and fantasies. Enter the space of **Awareness** of the **present moment** with no emotional filters, no regrets nor hopes, no daydreaming and no nightmares.

www.artof4elements.com

EXERCISE 1: TEN TINY CHANGES

This exercise is designed to strengthen the connection you have within your family and to develop the understanding of other human beings that share your heart, your home, your life.

Introduce ten tiny changes within the world of your relationship habits, beliefs or actions.

Record and remember 10 particular habits that occur within your relationship:

- With your parents
- With your siblings
- With your friends
- With your partners

For example:
- Your obsession to keep a particular door open at all times,
- The habit to go to the same place for croissant every day,
- Your habit to wear the same lipstick,
- Your habit to read the newspapers at the table,
- Your habit to say the exact same things to your children before they go to school,
- Your habit to do the exact same thing to your partner before s/he goes to work (a kiss, or no kiss, a hug, or no hugs)
- Squeeze the tooth-brush in exact the same way,

You get the point, identify any weird and wonderful habit that we all secretly and sub-consciously worship.

Change them and do them in a different way.

Surprise your partner, friends, parents or children.

Try to please other members of your family.

You can do it: secretly, openly or discreetly. Do not say to your partner what are the habits, patterns that you have changed, or that you are working on. The examples of these little treats for your family could be:

- Help your partner or child with the house chores. Do something that is usually done by the other family member. If a mum is the one to cook at all times, the son might decide to take this task; if it is the mother washes the clothes, father might decide to take this task for a moment.

- Buy a present to the family member, with no particular reason, buy some flowers, or socks to your dad.

- Prepare a bath for the tired partner, just when you know s/he is returning from a difficult day at work.

- Pick up your spouse from a day of work if she usually uses public transport to commute to and back from work, or go for your kids after school if they usually use the school bus to commute.

At the end of the week take some time to discuss the 'tiny' changes. Did you recognize the little presents that you have received during the week? How did you recognize the presents and how did you feel receiving these gifts to your patterns, habits and the way of life.

If you did not recognize the gifts, ask yourself why did this happen? What is it that I need to do differently so that my family member will recognize that I have changed something.

With these ten tiny changes, you will challenge the Master of Habits within your Mind that rules your Relationships and start exercising your Will Power towards more Love, Tolerance and Beauty within your life.

We also continue practicing Self-Remembering.

Mindful Being

'Our **mind** is constantly busy with thoughts and feelings about **our past, present or future**. To stop it from **useless chat**, we must learn how to hear this noise, become **aware of it**, and transform it through **concentration into mindfulness**.'

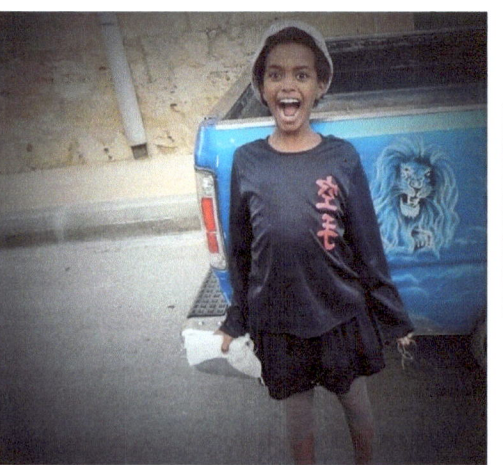

EXERCISE 2: ARE YOU TRULY LISTENING?

Ask yourself this question and stop for a moment to analyze your attitude towards the art of listening.

Do you like listening to others speak and encourage them to speak? Are you equally attentive to a friend, a neighbor, or a stranger. Do you focus on what the person is saying and are you cleat about the quality of conversation that you are having? Do you often interrupt the person who is speaking?

Use this exercise while you are trying to improve the relationships within your life. Active listening can do wonders.

Also, active listening will save you from a big Time Waster called Gossiping.

Be aware of Gossiping.

Do not Gossip.

There are so many other inspiring things to talk about than Talking About Other People...

RULES OF ACTIVE LISTENING
- keep quiet when the other one is talking
- ask related questions and listen to the answers
- show compassion whether with a stranger, neighbor or your shop-keeper

Mindful Being   by Nuit

When we say **Mind** we think of: **consciousness**, awareness, cognitive thinking; but also of: **intuition**, subconscious gibberish, or **unconscious strata** influencing our lives. The 'state' of this **Mind**, our **positive** or **negative** attitude towards the world, is closely related to our experiences of **happiness** or **suffering**.

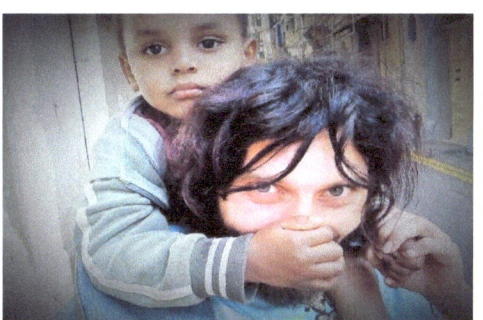

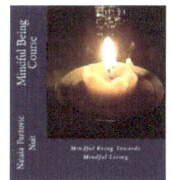

www.artof4elements.com

EXERCISE 3 EXERCISE CONSCIOUS SPEECH

EXERCISE 3A CHOSE A SUBJECT TO DEFEND OR ARGUE ABOUT DURING THE DAY

Chose a subject you usually get emotional about and de-touch from the feeling while you are defending your argument.

Stay behind the feeling.

Observe it.

Check the physical sensation of it.

Is it in the stomach?

Or in the chest?

Or perhaps it comes from the inspiration centre – from your throat?

Now, stop in the middle of your argument. Stop before you have finished it, let it go, no matter how passionate about it you might be.

Observe what happens to your body while you are exercising this conscious speech exercise.

EXERCISE 3B DEFEND SOMEBODY ELSE'S POINT OF VIEW

Defend somebody else's point of view even though you generally disagree with it.

Check how it feels to have the other person's point of view, argue it, defend it, work with it consciously.

EXERCISE 3C STOP IN THE MIDDLE OF AN ARGUMENT

If you argue with somebody today, stop in the middle of the argument.

Let it go.   Do not follow it any longer.   Do not pursue it.   Do not be right today.

Try to get out of this magic circle of unconscious behavior.

Be conscious of your words!

Tasks:

- T1 Meditate in the morning – learn to get in touch with silence within yourself

- T2 Set your clock ½ hour earlier and write a page of stream-of-consciousness writing. From today, do it every day for the next 6 weeks

EXERCISE 4: CIRCLE OF LOVE

HOW WELL DO YOU KNOW EACH OTHER

This exercise is designed to inspire you to get to know each other. Often we believe that we know things about our family members, and we take some basics for granted. This questionnaire will help you get closer to one another, you will start thinking about the other family member and you will become more harmonious as a group. Take an empty piece of paper and ask a number of questions. Answer the questions for yourself, for your partner, and for each of your family members. The questionnaire should look like the following table:

Question	My	My Partners	Kid 1	Kid 2
Favourite colour				
Favourite book				
Favourite poem				
Favouring meal				
Favourite flower				
Favourite crystal				
Favourite animal				
Favourite sport				
Biggest Fear				
Biggest Love / Inspiration				
Strongest Fun				
How to relax				
The best quality				
What do I do when I am happy				
What do I do when I am sad				
What others do when I am happy				
What others do when I am sad				
1 thing I would like to change				

Purified replacing Matter by Spirit
Cell by cell…
Nourished by **Earth**
Veiled by **Fire**
Carried by **Air**
Dissolved by **Water**
Filled with **God**
Intoxicated with God
Becoming Divine
Metal transformed into **Gold**
Through the supreme Magic of the mastery of
Thoughts and feelings
Evoking the **Infinite Wisdom** buried inside
Impeccably and non-compromising
Living the Infinite Love

Art of 4 Elements
by Nuit

Compare your notes and discuss them in a circle of love.

Circle of love has a rule that you can not criticize anybody's answers, you can not fight, you can not argue.

Circle of love is accepting, full of understanding, giving and loving.

Exercise 5: Your Relationship Plan

We should devote time to talk about our relationship, our true needs, and goals, what are the empowering things within the relationship that we are grateful for, and what we would like to change so that the relationship becomes stronger and more beautiful.

Take a note-book with your partner and spend some time answering the questions separately.

We are starting with the True Goals and True Purpose to keep your focus on what is really important.

- My ultimate Spiritual goal in life is:
    - For example: happiness as a state-of-being;
    - oneness with God
    - lightness of Being, etc.

- My purpose in Life is:
    - For example: to stay inspired and to inspire others
    - to live peacefully and stay healthy
    - to be in love with the world, etc.

- My mission in Life is:
    - For example: To reach my highest potential in everything I do
    - To raise my children as inspired and loving adults
    - To see God in all, etc.

- I wish to share my skills and beliefs with the World through:
    - For example: Giving Yoga Classes
    - Writing a book of poetry
    - The positive example to my kids and friends, etc.

- 5 most important things in my life are:
    - For example: Freedom
    - Love
    - Knowledge
    - Family and Friends
    - Union with God in meditation, prayer, etc.

What are the things I appreciate most in my relationship?

Where do I see this relationship going? What is our future?

What would I like to be able to do while in this relationship?

Body

- Walk the dogs together in the morning
- Have time to jog on my own in the afternoons

Emotions

- Develop an ability to cope with feelings openly and lovingly
- Avoid jealousy attacks
- Be truthful and honest about my feelings, needs, wants (devote time for sharing thoughts and feelings)

Thoughts

- wish to go back to school to acquire new business skills
- we could learn a new language together to add fun to our lives

Soul

- Devote space and time to developing deeper friendships
- Join a mantra singing or a prayer or a meditation group
- Take drawing classes on my-own / together to enhance creativity

What would I like to keep or change within this relationship?

- more time to be on my-own
- more time to do inspiring things together
- more freedom in my relationships with others
- wish you are not so critical / sarcastic, let's practice Positive Feedback together
- wish to have more time on my own while you are with the children

An addiction could become the number one value in our life. Many lose things that are extremely important to their addictions to food, drinking, work, drugs, sex, gambling, shopping, etc.

Write down this sentence:

- If you would quit _____, I would be able to _____.

While analyzing the questions and answers together, be open and honest, work with the essence, don't let the trivial distract you. For example, have you ever heard a statement...

- If I had more money, I could holiday more often. Then I could spend more quality time with my family and friends

In this statement, the problem is not money, but the luck of quality time together. Find ways to enhance your time together.

At the end of the exercise, create a list of concrete actions that are a result of this exchange with your partner and add them to your Life.

Repeat this exercise every 6 months or a year.

Relationships Article: Chemistry of Love: Is true love forever

Relationships and Chemistry - What is Love

'Look at every path closely and deliberately, then ask ourselves this crucial question: Does this path have a heart? If it does, then the path is good. If it doesn't, it is of no use.' **Carlos Castaneda**

If you are anything like me, even just a mention of words: **falling in love, love and sex** will inspire the motion of the magic potion of **Oxytocin** (Greek: ōkytokínē, meaning 'quick birth') in your brain.

Join the crowd of all of us, mortals, artists, poets, spiritual teachers, singers, all, that try their very best to understand this amazing mix that keeps our eyes sparkling, our hearts warm, and our relationships healthy.

Applying the law of attraction (you will attract into your life whatever you focus on) to the subject of spiritual relationship, we all dream to move into a space of abundance of love, abundance of passion and abundance of understanding. However, we are so heavily conditioned by the concept of soul-mates and tied within ferry-tales subconscious chains that we find it difficult to **clearly observe love**, and the above drive somehow manages to escape our focus and sometimes even manages to miss our lives.

Oxytoxin - your magic love hormone

So, if exploring relationships as a spiritual path is your quest too, let's together try to unveil Venus and gain some more insights into her enchantment. Let's look at her purely scientifically, observing the chemical changes that occur within our bodies while we love or are in love, let's have a quick glance at the studies that explore the laboratory of our brain.

Let us first meet **Oxytocin**, a hormone and neurotransmitter, also known as the 'love hormone'. Oxytocin is linked to the feelings of love, empathy, and connection to others, it makes us feel content, it encourages human bonding, and trust. The primary conscious behavior that increases oxytocin is caring for another. In 2003, a study showed that oxytocin levels in the blood increases after a session of cuddling; oxytocin is involved in the initiation of maternal behavior inducing labor and milk ejection; oxytocin spikes up just after an orgasm and it actually causes spontaneous erections in rats. So it is no wonder that after making love, with the level of oxytocin in our blood, we believe we can not live without our partner, we bond with him/her, and we have cravings for the person.

We all form similar deep connections with our loved ones. **Oxytocin** is the chemical reason behind the love induced behaviors, but it also shapes our health and our happiness - it is said that people with pets tend to recover more quickly from illness, that married people tend to live longer, that love can heal drugs addictions...

Falling in love calls forth a mix of neuro-chemicals, including oxytocin's bonding effects. Falling in love also calls forth the Lady Lust that is our craving for sex.

How to Train Love Conscious Relationships

A study of brain activity in 2000 examined students that were madly in love scanning their brains. The interesting finding was that 'love', in its euphoria, uses the same neural mechanisms activated during taking drugs. Remember, those feelings of excitement, butterflies in your stomach, the intrusive & somewhat obsessive thoughts about the loved ones... Some analysts suggests that the actual behavioral **patterns of those 'in love' resemble obsessive compulsive disorder** :) The mix of chemicals responsible for this turmoil includes increases in the levels of **serotonin**, and **oxytocin**.

LOVE VS FALLING IN LOVE

Love and falling in love are independent mechanisms and can work independently or simultaneously. It is no news that a human can have a loving and understanding relationship with his long-term partner, while feeling lust or romantic love for someone else. Most people act this scenario with a heap of confusion, jealousy, and adultery that leads to divorce. A normal relationship pattern is for couples to fall in love, get together, promise they will love each other forever, and after 5-10 years end up getting bored of each other. Unfortunately, over time, the roller coaster of highs and lows of a relationship creates a distance between partners. Our obsession with day-to-day worries makes us forget the magic of love.

Love with its sexual and spiritual energy is an amazingly precious energy and with its proper use **we can enter the space of inner peace, passionate creativity, sparkling health, and life balance**. Love is nature's most precious drug that actually shapes how we view the world. The more we spread love and connect with our surroundings, the more responsive our body and brain becomes to it.

So what do you think, what is the recipe for producing more oxytocin? My main guess would be: let's train love... let's practice tantra... let's exercise carrying... let's fall in love, every day, with Life... And yours?

EXERCISE 6: EXPRESS FREEDOM

This exercise is here so that we can express our gratitude towards the quality of FREEDOM. Even within a relationship we should still have our 'breathing space', we should still experience a 'sense of freedom', and enjoy 'doing things on our own'.

Compose an aria with a title 'Freedom'

Write a poem with a subject 'Freedom'

Draw a painting called 'Freedom'

Plan and execute a Freedom day in a month or in a week.

EXERCISE 7: EXPRESS LOVE

Compose an aria with a title 'Love

Write a poem with a subject 'Love

Draw a painting called 'Love

Plan and execute a Love day in a month or in a week.

Tasks:

- T1 Meditate in the morning – learn to get in touch with silence within yourself

- T2 Set your clock ½ hour earlier and write a page of stream-of-consciousness writing. From today, do it every day for the next 6 weeks

SEX AND LONG TERM RELATIONSHIPS - WHY DO WE STOP HAVING SEX?

Initially, winning a partner with the most desirable genes was one of the reasons why we went out to seek partner and why we offered sex. The sexual game soon became connected with the excitement, passion, and bliss of 'falling in love', entered our fairytales, became part of our conscious and sub-conscious make-up, and waged chemical wars within our brains. So, the question What is Love? became very complex to answer. Today, most people aspire to obtain lifelong love, and most people wish to have a fulfilling sexual relationship. So, the statistic of the estimated 20 million married couples in America living in sexless marriages (sex less than ten times a year) comes as quite shocking.

Nikola Tesla, St. Teresa of Avila or Sri Aurobindo would wholeheartedly tell you that they have deliberately avoided sex and relationships to preserve energy and to safeguard it for the fulfilment of their mission – their mental work or their spiritual growth. Most major religions will support this decision because in their viewpoint sexual energy belongs to our animal nature, is used for reproduction, and should be left sleeping within the realms of our sub-conscious.

Taoist and **Tantrist** tend to differ from this main-stream religious approach to sex.

SEX AND LONG TERM RELATIONSHIPS - TAOISTS AND JOINING THE ESSENCES

During the Han Dynasty that ruled from 200BC to 200AC, Taoists were performing sexual intercourse as a spiritual practice. In China, they have developed various sexual practices also known as: 'joining of the essences' that lead their practitioners to good health, longevity, and immortality. The essence of their teaching was in the preservation of sperm because they linked the sperm loss to the loss of the vital life force. According to the Taoist, meditation is an important part of the sexual merge, and the lovers intentionally direct the life energy into the brain.

For an expert Taoist view, please have a look at Mantak Chia's book: 'Taoist Secrets of Love'.

In an interview with Lama Tantrapa, Lama talks about the sexual energy as the most powerful energyk: 'Jing qi, or sexual energy, is the most powerful energy we have. It is like "baby formula" for the spirit.' Following his pursuit, he suggests that Taoist students should live a puritan life-style taking care of their life force: 'Sex, drugs, even coffee...these cause a loss of energy, even though an addict feels listless without them...after experiencing the bliss of practice, these addictions will lose their hold.'

TANTRIC SHIVA AND SHAKTI MERGE

India was the birth-place of the esoteric teaching of Tantra and Tantra was practiced by a small number of Hindus and Buddhists practitioners. A tantric sexual merge maithuna is used by the practitioners to nurture the sexual energy and achieve union with the divine, and it is only one aspect of this elaborate spiritual practice.

Osho Rajneesh, a contemporary tantric master that lived during the last century, says: 'Unless your sexuality rises and reaches to love it is mundane, it has nothing sacred about it. When your sex becomes love, then it is entering into a totally different dimension — the dimension of the mysterious and the miraculous.'

Both Taoist and Tantrics advocate sexual union that lasts for hours.

MYSTICAL LINK BETWEEN SEXUALITY AND LOVE

The sacred texts give us an idea of how we could treat this mystical link between sexuality and love, and between sexuality and spirituality.

The modern psychologists are still struggling to unravel this amazing puzzle of conscious and un-conscious phenomena living within the twilight zone of sexuality.

Why do we have sex? Or if it is so good, why do we stop having sex? A research done by **Meston and Buss** involving more than a 1,000 people, gives us some insight into how many people link sex and love. They have interviewed people from all over the world asking them: why do you have sex?

According to a research

TOP 10 REASONS WOMEN HAVE SEX ARE

1. I was attracted to the person
2. I wanted to experience physical pleasure
3. It feels good
4. I wanted to show my affection to the person
5. I wanted to express my love for the person
6. I was sexually aroused and wanted the release
7. I was 'horny'
8. It's fun
9. I realized I was in love
10. I was 'in the heat of the moment'

TOP 10 REASONS MEN HAVE SEX ARE

1. I was attracted to the person.
2. It feels good.
3. I wanted to experience the physical pleasure.
4. It's fun.
5. I wanted to show my affection to the person.
6. I was sexually aroused and wanted the release.
7. I was "horny."
8. I wanted to express my love for the person.
9. I wanted to achieve an orgasm.
10. I wanted to please my partner.

BREAKING STEREOTYPES

The stereotype 'women do it for love, and men for joy' does not quite win the argument. Both men and women seem to seek love and pleasure out of the sexual intercourse. Within the book, you can find some most amusing quotes, such as: 'Most of the time I just lie there and make lists in my head. I grunt once in a while so he knows I'm awake, and then I tell him how great it was when it's over. We are happily married.'

Within a long-term relationship, as time goes by, one loses the initial spark and desires wane and one stops having as much sex. It could be that the brain gets accustomed to all the inflow of the chemicals or one simply gets bored of the partner, the result is – no sex. Keeping the intimacy and attraction between partners becomes 'work' or as Taoists and Tantrists call it - a 'spiritual practice'. We suggest to all that might have this problem, to start their 'work' or 'spiritual practice', immediately, further exploring the ancient tools and techniques, because the deepest and the most fulfilling closeness between partners comes from the intimacy of this long-term effort of understanding sexuality and transforming an unconscious sexual intercourse into maithuna.

SEXUAL EVOLUTION: CULTURAL REVOLUTION THAT IS STILL TO HAPPEN

LOVE AND SEX - BACK IN TIME

Condemnations of fornication can be found in every epoch. While it was OK for a man to pursue sexual opportunity, all across the globe, a woman was supposed to be much more virtuous. Only a bit more than one hundred years ago, we lived in a world where the idea of a woman's sexual freedom seemed unthinkable.

Going back in time, In England between the 13th and 16th centuries, extramarital sex was policed to such an extend that up to 90% of the court cases handled by the Church was about adultery, sodomy and prostitution. A woman was the property of fathers and husbands so if she had sex with a stranger, her family felt that a crime was committed against them.

By 1900, Freud published his Interpretation of Dreams, and put in place the stage for the sexual revolution. Twenty years later, his student **Wilhelm Reich**, who was a sexual evangelist of the time, published his study 'The Function of the Orgasm', that publically claimed that 'there is only one thing wrong with neurotic patients: the lack of full and repeated sexual satisfaction'

ORGONE ENERGY ACCUMULATOR

Even though Dr. Reich's books were burned in Germany he managed to find a fertile ground for his experiments in the US. He invented and presented to his curious audience - the Orgone Energy Accumulator - a six-sided box, with a look and feel of a small sauna, that accumulated sexual energy. Reich saw sexuality as the primary energetic force of life. The term - Orgone - shares its root with the word orgasm, that he believed is a fundamental expression of a person's psychological health. Reich believed that the natural flow of life-energy in the body can be blocked, leading to physical and mental diseases. He believed that his invention collects energy and that its mysterious currents can cure sickness and restore the life force. His Orgone box became a symbol of the sexual revolution. During his time, Reich and his students were accused of being a 'cult of sex and anarchy,'

REVOLUTION & EVOLUTION

It was not until the 1970s that women's sexual activity outside the marriage was accepted. The young generation of the 1960s that questioned authority and rejected their parents' values, and the distribution of contraceptives (Enovid, the first birth control pill, went on the market in 1960) shaped the course of the revolution. The birth-control pill gave people a choice to have children when they wanted them and the use of condoms protected the couples from sexually transmitted diseases. This was the time of much needed social change, the change that was echoed within all spheres of life, we started to have nudity on TV, and pornography became a part of our society, we were changing out civil rights laws, we witnessed the women's liberation movement, and the fight for gay & lesbian rights. The moral revolution started transforming every dimension of our life.

Does Virginity Matter? or Cultural Change that is still to happen

The cultural revolution is yet to happen, it will take place when the idea crystallizes and gains its grip within various cultures. Around the world, the sexual freedom still needs some time to become our reality. In some parts of the world, women are still abused because of their sexuality: their clitorises are cut, their bodies are fully covered, they are raped, or stoned for the sin of 'fornication'.

Every year, thousands of Chinese women pay around $700 for an operation to restore their hymens shortly before their wedding so that their husbands can see blood on the sheets on their honeymoon night. To many Chinese, virginity matters even though the percentage of Chinese women who admit to engage in premarital sex is now around 50. Sex is simultaneously suppressed and commoditized. Its expression is both hidden and blatantly manifested. The talk of 'sin' is still part of our conscious and subconscious make-up and 'shame and blame' game can still manifest in chains and control of many.

Within the next stage of this fascinating revolution, we will learn more about our sex and sexuality, more about our-own way to act or re-act to a sexual impulse, we will learn how to distinguish between love and sexual attraction, about **falling in love**, and our chemical responses to the love game, and learn more about energies and its use to stay healthy and happy.

Sexual intimacy makes us vulnerable to our partner and it requires trust and love. Hopefully, the next stage of this evolution will also bring us honesty as an equal partner to the sexual drive, honesty when choosing the sexual partner that we can trust, and invite into our lives, honesty toward our-own-selves and others.

Relationship and Sexual Hygiene

Sexual hygiene and honeymoon

How many young couples during the 'honeymoon' days of falling in love and at the beginning of their relationship stop to talk about their sexual health? To get to know one another they will go through many different questions: how many partners have you had, and what did you eat for breakfast when you were 8 – this still stays an interesting part of a mating game, but rarely they ask – how many times have you had unprotected sex and who was it with? Because this question is not asked, our society still has an enormous number of: teenage pregnancies, abortions, cancers, and sexually transmitted diseases.

Sexual Hygiene and Unprotected Sex

Do we really need to talk about condoms, now, 400 years after their introduction and after they have won almost all the ticks & approvals from health professionals, governments, or anybody with a bit of brain or common sense? I say, almost all, because unfortunately there are still some segments of medical community and religious watchdogs that consider sexually transmitted diseases to be God's punishment for sexual misbehaviour and the use of condoms immoral.

Do we need to talk about condoms even though it is widely accepted that they should be used for the prevention of sexually transmitted diseases and they are freely sold in super-markets, & pubs, and used by millions? The answer is yes, we still need to talk about condoms as long as this 'necessary nuisance' does not become part of our upbringing, day-to-day life, and conditioning, like food… or wearing clothes… or putting lipstick when going out… checking our pockets for condoms…

Having in mind the amount of disease that can be caused by unprotected sex, I will ask you a question - how many of you, female readers, practice to carry condoms in your purse, going out for a wild Saturday night? How many of you, male readers, would think that a woman who carry condoms in her purse is a whore? And how many of you had a thought just before the first sexual act with a new partner – 'if I insist on the condom business right now, I will spoil this precious moment' or 'the fact that I am letting him into myself without protection, shows that I care for him and trust him enough to do so' or 'if I have a condom handy right now, it will show that I was 'getting ready' for sex all along and this will ruin my 'hunting game'.

SEXUAL HYGIENE: CAMPAIGNS PROMOTING PROTECTED SEX

In March 2010, the Swiss Government created a campaign promoting smaller condoms intended for teenagers. They realized that due to the fact that standard condoms are too wide, adolescent boys refused to use them and so bringing themselves into a grave danger. I haven't heard of many other Governments that followed this progressive initiative even though it is well known that the use of condoms reduces the risk of AIDS transmission by 85%.

A study published in **The Journal of Sexual Medicine** with the findings of National Survey of Sexual Health and Behavior in the US in 2010 reports that amongst unmarried adults condoms were used during one-third of recent sexual intercourse. According to the data, men (both adolescent and adult) consistently report more condom use than women. The same magazine reported that Latino women living in the US are often even afraid to bring up the subject of condom use with their partners…

So my dear female and male readers, let me ask you another question - how many of you have had unprotected sex with a stranger at least once in your life-time? And if you haven't, how many of you dream to have this one night with a stranger, that is wild, sexy, unpredictable, and how many times in your imagination, you put a condom on the erected penis, to protect yourself? So we still need to talk about condoms…

PERFECT SEXUAL HEALTH

Now, let us together imagine a society where at no circumstances one will have sex with a new partner unless s/he has done all the tests – HIV, etc. I can almost hear your thoughts, isn't that far too strict? Ok, but how else can we determine how serious one is with his or her sexual hygiene? When exactly can you trust a man to tell you that he has wards – after 1 day or 10 days of knowing him, after a month, or two? And a woman, when can you trust a woman to tell you that she has wards? Will she ever tell you, or stay ashamed of it to such an extent that this will stay only her little secret? How many young couples during the 'honeymoon' days of falling in love and at the beginning of their relationship stop to talk about their sexual hygiene? To get to know one another they will go through many different questions: how many partners have you had, and what did you eat for breakfast when you were 8 – this still stays an interesting part of a mating game, but rarely they ask – how many times have you had unprotected sex and who was it with? Because this question is not asked, our society still has an enormous number of: teenage pregnancies, abortions, cancers, and sexually transmitted diseases.

I invite you to become a part of this 'perfect' society where sexual hygiene is taken very seriously, where a man takes care of his sexual health, not leaving it to a chance that a woman he is in love with is of a 'conscious' sort. I invite you to become a woman that has plenty of courage and love and respect for her body and uses condoms regularly religiously. I invite both of you to get acquainted with all the different little rubbery tools that might be helpful during the sexual game. Explore different condoms, include the likes of femidom in your list of possessions - a female condom - that will give a woman a possibility to fully control her sexual health. Stay free, conscious and ready to take the responsibility of your body and sexual act, and when you go out next time, do not hesitate, put into your pocket your condom or femidom and have a wonderful night of fun...

TRANSFORMATION TOOLS ALCHEMY OF LOVE

MODULE 8 OUR GREATER SURROUNDING

Our Highest Potential is Waiting

We live in our greater surrounding and when we become conscious and aware, our capability for love grows and expands into our surroundings – Earth, animals, plants, strangers…

QUESTIONNAIRE 1 OUR GREATER SURROUNDING

This questionnaire contains a number of words that describe your attitude to your greater surrounding, your attitude towards Earth, animals, strangers.

Read each item and rate them from 1 (lowest) to 5 (highest). Answer to what extent you feel this way right now, that is, at the present moment.

- I take care of Earth because we are too nature

- I recycle, I use as little plastic as possible, I eat organics, I am vegetarian, etc.

- I am grateful for every day and I express my thanks to people that surround me

- I love animals and take care of them whenever I can

- I am never too busy to help a friend

- I support various NGOs in their work to help Earth, Animals, Poor

- I am active in my Local Council, my Building Council working on the better environment

- I actively support environmental protection initiatives

- I help in my children School's voluntary activities

- I try to understand rather than judge people who are accused of being wrong

WRITE THE ANSWERS OF THE PERSONALITY QUESTIONNAIRE

ALCHEMY OF LOVE COURSE   MODULE 8 OUR GREATER SURROUNDING   QUESTIONNAIRE 1

Date_____   Name_____

Our Greater Surrounding	1	2	3	4	5
1 I take care of Earth because we are too nature					
2 I recycle, I use as little plastic as possible, I eat organics, I am vegetarian, etc.					
3 I am grateful for every day and I express my thanks to people that surround me					
4 I love animals and take care of them whenever I can					
5 I am never too busy to help a friend					
6 I support various NGOs in their work to help Earth, Animals, Poor					
7 I am active in my Local Council, my Building Council working on the better environment					
8 I actively support environmental protection initiatives					
9 I help in my children School's voluntary activities					
10 I do charity work					

My List of Priorities: Items Marked as 1, 2 and 3 are:

Our Greater Surroundings	1	2	3

Page 156

Write down the areas that need improvement. Be specific...

For example:

- I very much wish to be kind, loving and giving to my fellow human beings but the opportunity never shows up

- I am too busy to join any NGO

- The world is too f...cked up that an individual effort is useless

Change these into positive attitudes and create A WORLD OF YOUR DREAMS…

God created **Nature**
Full of **Chaos**
Where no two things are **Equal**
Where no sound, no colour,
no shape is repeated.
Man copied God and created
Symmetry, **Mathematics**,
Music, Straight Lines
Man copied God and created
Perfection.
Together Man-made perfect elements create
an Absolute Disorder
Together God-made **imperfections** result in an
Ultimate Harmony.

Perfection by **Nuit** Art of 4 Elements

photo: Minja Gutic

Exercise 1 Change the Word

Within this exercise you will write answers on the following questions about the environment and your relationship with Gaia.

I like animals because _____

I like plants because _____

I think that Earth is _____

If my friend dirty the environment I would _____

When people smoke next to me, I tell them _____

When I think of healthy nutrition I think of _____

When I think about health the most important is that I _____

When I think of a healthy planet, we would need to _____

When I think of happy animals I think of _____

You can change the world

EXERCISE 2 | HAVE THE POWER TO CHANGE THE WORLD

If you have a possibility to open an NGO, what is the NGO that you would create?

Would you work on your own or with your friends, what type of activity would you include within the work of such an organization; what are the areas that your NGO would cover?

This exercise is designed to create an awareness of all the things one can do to help protect our Mother Earth from destruction.

EXERCISE 2: SERVICE

Any act of service, performed in a spirit of unconditional giving, expands the qualities of compassion, love, and tolerance. You will learn to serve Divine through the people you are helping.

Make sure you help someone every day this week.

Be more attentive to other people's needs and you will see that there are many ways to help. Ask them do they need your help, or just go and do it.

Your service could be done for animals or environment you are living in.

We are all part of the same Life Force...

Tasks: T1 Meditate in the morning – learn to get in touch with silence within yourself

- T2 Set your clock ½ hour earlier and write a page of stream-of-consciousness writing. From today, do it every day for the next 6 weeks

TRANSFORMATION TOOLS ONLINE LIFE COACHING

MODULE 9 YOUR DREAMS

Turn away from your dream and it will come back to you. Follow it and it will give you a tremendous amount of pleasure and learning.

Life is what we make of it.

Our dreams become our reality.

Our reality becomes the world we are all living in.

Addictions and habits do not support our Dreams. They bring us back to Instincts, Laziness, and they keep on ruining our health and wellbeing. They are usually very expensive.

Consumption of alcohol, drugs, smoking, impulsive shopping, over-eating, sugar addiction, eating too much junk food, wasting time on TV, computer games, laziness, worry, constant messaging , keeping unnecessary items instead of getting rid of them, lying for no reason, being a workaholic, etc. They all stay our little burdens that keep hold of our lives.

Getting rid of your instinctive behavior strengthens your willpower to change and to take responsibility within your life.

Exercise 1 Identify Your True Dreams

Want - What is it exactly that you want / that are your priorities in life? What activities do I love to do in my free time? What is it that I loved doing before, as a kid or before I had kids?

For Your Body:

- Is it a sane mind, Is it a stronger body, Is it a healthier body
- Is it more money

For Your Mind

- Is it more love
- Is it less anger / hatred / struggle with fears
- Is it more time to play, be creative, laugh with friends

For Your Soul

- Do you know how to listen to your soul
- Do you meditate / pray
- Do you write, Do you draw, Do you dance

For Your Family

- Do you respect Rhythm
- Do you give enough space for Love
- Do you respect Freedom

EXERCISE 1A I PERFORM (UN)HAPPILY

This exercise should be done with your partner, if you have one.

Make a list of activities that you do willingly and happily and the list on the opposite side of the table that you do unhappily. For example you can put within your list things like: I do not like talking to anybody in the morning, I do not like when TV is on when I talk to somebody, I dislike when you read newspapers or answer your mobile when we eat together, I do not like cleaning after you.

You could try exchanging with your partner or with your children the activities that you perform unhappily.

If you do not like washing dishes consider exchanging this duty for any other your partner performs unhappily for a week.

Do have in mind that some of the 'chores' just simply need to be done and if you suffer doing them, perhaps you can find a way to do this activity 'mindfully'.

Can I change anything within this list?

EXERCISE 2 YOUR IMAGINARY LIVES

If you had a chance to do it all over again, to be re-born again, imagine the lives you would live. What would you be: a priest, a yogi, an actor, a male, a female, a businessman, a teacher, a healer, a scientist?

Write down whatever comes to your mind, whatever new circumstances excite you, whatever new successes would intrigue you, whatever qualities of these imaginary lives would inspire you.

QUESTIONNAIRE 1 YOUR TRUE DREAMS

Let us ask your soul about your True Dreams. Answer to what extent you feel this way right now.

- I have adequate time to do what I want in my life
- I have adequate finances to do what I want in my life
- I have adequate energy to do what I want in my life
- I have balance between work and leisure to fully participate in life
- I love spending time in nature and I have enough time and energy to do so
- Spirituality means lot to me and I spend enough time in my spiritual pursuits
- Achieving something valuable for my Soul _____ is the highest goal in life
- I am excited when I learn something new and I created time and space for new learning adventures
- I find the world to be a very interesting and inspiring place. I have fun exploring its wonders
- My work is productive and inspiring and my work environment is healthy
- I have a loving relationship with my friends and family. I spend enough time with them.
- I love horse-riding, drawing, football _____, and I created time and space for my passion

ADD YOUR OWN QUESTIONS.

Spiritual Journey Learn to Listen to Your Soul

Body Mind Soul
Train Love   **Train Willpower**
Respect Gaia   **Respect Life**
Respect Silence
Conscious Living
Mindful Eating   **Mindful Being**
Conscious Relationships

Mindfulness Training

MINDFUL BEING COURSE   MODULE 9 YOUR DREAMS   QUESTIONNAIRE 1

Date_____   Name_____

Your True Dreams	1	2	3	4	5
1 I have adequate time in my life to do what I want to					
2 I have balance between work and leisure to fully participate in life					
3 I love spending time in nature and I have enough time and energy to do so					
4 Spirituality means lot to me and I spend enough time in my spiritual pursuits					
5 Achieving something valuable for my Soul is the highest goal in life					

My List of Priorities Items Marked as 1, 2 and 3 are:

My True Dreams	1	2	3

ACTION ITEM FROM THE PERSONALITY QUESTIONNAIRE

Study each answer that you are not happy with and determine what precise action you would like to do to change your state of body, mind, emotions.

Write down the areas that need improvement. Be specific...

- More quality time with my family – family meal once a day

- Time to be silent, to read, to walk - wake up 1 hour earlier to meditate and do the soul's diary

- Create time for friends, for deeper contacts and meaningful socializing

- Develop my skills to successfully start working on my long term plans in life

- Creating time to express love through play and laughter

To achieve my highest potential and the highest potential of my family I will:

Be Specific: about time,

> **quantity and**

>> **quality of activity that will change**

> **your body, mind and**

allow your soul to express fulfilling your highest potential.

While creating your action list for True Dreams to become your reality, have in mind two things:

GRATITUDE   Be grateful for what you already have

IMPROVEMENT   Constantly improve, learning new ways to Love and Be

Be creative, be honest. This list should now become your Action List. Do whatever you can to change uninspiring to inspiring, chaotic to harmonious, confused to balanced, irritated to loving…

Mindfulness & Conscious Being

MINDFUL BEING COURSE	MODULE 9 TRUE DREAMS	IDENTIFY TRUE DREAMS

Date_____		Name_____

Living my Dreams	Emotional Consequence	Positive Alternative / Action Items

Tasks:

- T1 Meditate in the morning – learn to get in touch with silence within yourself

- T2 Set your clock ½ hour earlier and write a page of stream-of-consciousness writing. From today, do it every day for the next 6 weeks

TRANSFORMATION TOOLS ALCHEMY OF LOVE

Module 10 Your True Goals

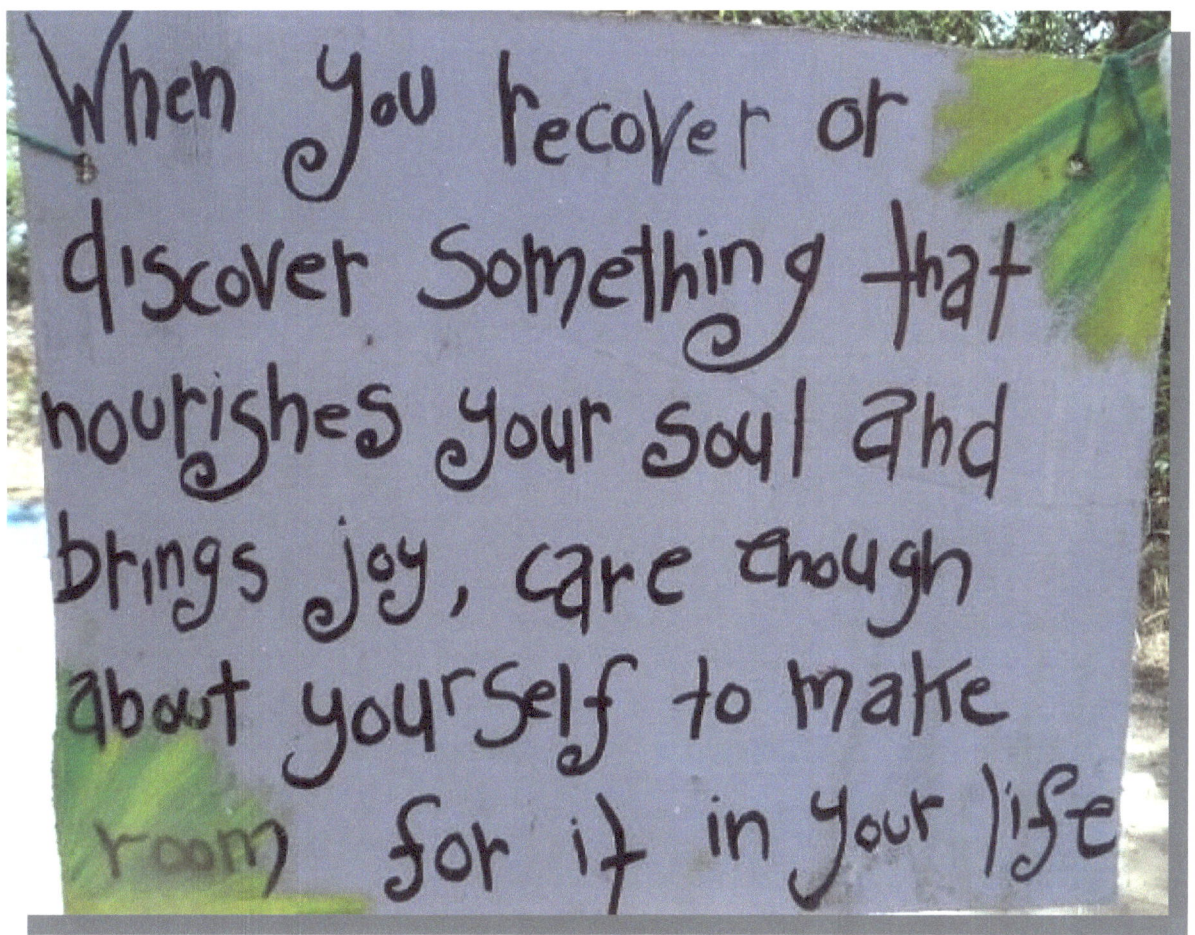

Our True Goal Is To…

- ❖ Inspire, motivate, and encourage…

What is Your?

To help you with your **True Goal** write down:

1. Who are the people I admire? What are their qualities and what is it that I admire? Write at least 7 names.

2. What is the book that left the most impression on me? Can the main characters tell me something about my Goals?

- What is it that touched me so deeply?

- What is it within me that resonate with the main message of the book?

3. What is the film that inspired me most? What is the reason for it?

4. Is there a business or career that would help me do what I love to do?

5. Is there a hobby that I should keep that would help me do what I love to do?

Now, find a quiet place, sit down and write down your true goals, write down:

- My True Goals are…

Do bigger and bolder – this is your Highest Potential Dream - go beyond your comfort zone

Exercise 1   Your Personal Development Plan

A good self development plan is a journey, an ongoing process of personal development. Write your main skills, your main qualities, your main interest... Make a drawing of it, make it FUN and color each area as it first comes to your Mind. Your Soul will talk to you through Colors.

The following are the questions you need to answer to be able to build your personal development plan:

1. Where are you right now?

2. Where do you want to be?

3. What are your core strengths?

4. What are your Weaknesses / Improvement areas?

5. Write down your Core Beliefs...

6. What are your Short-Term Plans / Goals?

7. What are your Long-Term Goal? What is the purpose to which you wish to devote the rest of your life?

8. List a number of Short Term Actions / Milestones for achieving your Long Term Goal

9. What are your Goals and Actions for the next year?

10. What are your Goals and Actions for the longer term?

Create action items: Small and Big Ones. These actions need not to be perfect, you will fine tune them as you go along.

Date_____   Name_____

Identify Your Goals	Identify Actions to Achieve Goals	Time-Scale	Resources
Short-term			
Short-term			
Medium-term			
Medium-term			
Long-term			
Long-term			

COMMITMENT: DISCIPLINE YOURSELF TO DO YOUR ACTIONS

Your action will become your **inspiration**. If you are happy and having fun, you take care of your Body, Mind and Soul, your creativity will flourish, and the end result will always be more fun and more happiness.

Doing something simply because everyone else is doing it, or because your loved ones think it is the best for you, will not help you to reach your highest potential. What is truly important to you as an individual, what flows with your strengths and weaknesses, what inspires you most? Be honest with the answers, seek clarity and your Soul will show you your purpose.

If your heart and your mind are not in-tuned they will become opposing forces within your life. The mind will constantly be saying, 'I have to do this now...' but your heart will stop it, saying: 'I am not enjoying this, let's leave it for tomorrow'. Within this game of opposites we will become lazy, over-loaded with work that we are not finishing, and we will end up feeling unhappy.

If we are using pure will-power to fight our heart, we will become tired very quickly, but if we are using our Heart's strengths, its inspiration, passion and calling, these two opposing forces will act in Union to produce SUPER results. So, sit in a quiet place, go deep into your meditative state, and write, write whatever comes to your Mind. The answer that makes you feel inspired, peaceful and fulfilled is the one you are looking for.

Draw it! Have FUN with IT! Stick IT on your Kitchen Board! And NOW Live IT!

Transformation tools Alchemy of Love

Module 11 What is Spirituality?

What is Karma?

What is Karma?

Karma is a set of actions and reactions that are interconnected, a set of cause and effects that form a Natural Universal Law and are operating in the realm of human life. A person is affected by his or her thoughts, emotions and actions.

Karma could be:

- National

- Inherited from parents

- Caused by a set of incarnations if you believe in incarnation

Each person's karma interacts, exchanges, influences each other

'For the only decree of **Karma** - an eternal and immutable decree - is absolute Harmony in the world of matter as it is in the world of Spirit. It is not, therefore, Karma that rewards or punishes, but it is we, who reward or punish ourselves according to whether we work with, through and along with nature, abiding by the laws on which that Harmony depends, or - break them.' (Secret Doctrine, Blavatsky)

'**Karma**... One of the most important of the laws of nature. Ceaseless in its operation, it bears alike upon planets, systems of planets, races, nations, families, and individuals. It is the twin doctrine to reincarnation. So inextricably interlaced are these two laws that it is almost impossible to properly consider one apart from the other. No spot or being in the universe is exempt from the operation of Karma, but all are under its sway, punished for error by it yet beneficently led on, through discipline, rest, and reward, to the distant heights of perfection. It is a law so comprehensive in its sweep, embracing at once our physical and our moral being.' (Ocean Of Theosophy Ocean William Q. Judge p. 89)

Exercise 1   So What is Karma For You?

Exercise 2: Your Spiritual Diary

The **Spiritual Diary** let us focus our energies towards important things in our lives – creativity, virtues, righteousness, inspiring writings, spiritual company, God.

Spiritual Diary is a great help within the spiritual path.

Spiritual Diary is there to remind you of what is important and it is there so you can avoid the horrible time-wasters that keep occupying our hours / days / weeks / months – TV, Computer, Gossiping, Fearful Thinking – that keep us away from spending time within the creative flow.

You will keep the spiritual diary every day, continuously, for two months. This method was included within the teaching of many spiritual masters.

You will record the time spent in spiritual practices. Devoting regular time to the Spiritual Practices is an indication that your curiosity towards Spirit and your relationship with Spirit is widening and deepening.

The *spiritual diary* is very sacred. It should always be a true reflection of your inner state.

Spiritual Diary is there to help you identify problems and inspirations on your spiritual path. After some time, you will answer the questions such as: Is my meditation improving? Is my capacity for love growing? Is my self-confidence increasing? Do I allow myself enough creative time to be able to flourish?

If your day is truly disappointing and you realize that you lied and cheated and wasted your time and energy, you will stay aware of this fact and will change tomorrow. If you told lies today, don't tell them tomorrow. This is very simple!

When you keep diary, you practice the attention. We remember only if our attention is there, only if we are awake. That is why we do not remember what we've done only a week ago, how did we spend our days...

Spiritual & Creative Diary   **Month………**

Questions   Dates

Physical Body

When did I get up from bed?

When did I go to sleep?

Mark for your sleep / dream

What is the physical exercise that I've done?

- walking

- running

- any individual or collective sport…

Mark for your physical activity today

Food & Drink Quality

Food & Drink Quantity

Mark for your nutritional intake

Spiritual & Creative Diary   **Month………**

Questions   Dates

Mental Body

How long did I meditate

- in the morning, during the day, in the evening

What is the noise level around me (noise from TV, Radio, etc.)

Did I read any spiritual book today?

Did I spend time with the wise and inspiring people?

Did I do any selfless service today?

How much time have I spent in a creative activity?

- Writing

- Drawing, Story Telling…

How much time did I spend in nature / with nature

Spiritual & Creative Diary   **Month........**

Questions   Dates

Emotional Body

How much time did I spend with friends / loved ones in a good quality exchange

Have I made love today, or have I fallen into sex today

Time spent with useless company / activity

- Gossiping, TV / Games / Social Media
- Worrying, fighting, arguing

Time spent doing nothing / worrying

My Children

Quality time spent with my children

Did I follow the routine vs. freedom with my children today?

Shouting, screaming, scolding

Laughing, playing, exploring

Spiritual & Creative Diary   Month……..

Questions   Dates

My Soul

What are the virtues that I am developing consciously?

Non Violence

Truthfulness

Lightness of being – healthy humor

Love

Prayer

EXERCISE 3 DRUMMING, MEDITATION, YOGA CIRCLE

Join a drumming circle, a meditation circle or start going to yoga.

Sing mantras and devotional songs… Singing is **healing**

Sing songs that are inspiring, that are created to help humankind or a personal growth.

Feeling the vibration of the sound is a sacred and profound experience. It is a form of Bhakti Yoga. It needs the proper breathing, proper relaxation, and proper state of mind. Chanting [mantras](#) properly, your being starts to shine, your soul finds the way to express itself through sounds and your heart opens.

Through the chanting we develop our relationship with Divine

Join a Mantra Chanting Circle or a Drumming Circle!

Indigenous cultures practiced circle drumming for thousands of years. If you can not join a Drumming Circle in your neighborhood, form your own Circle, join together with friends and explore the magic of jamming.

Respect the sacredness of the drumming rituals. Drumming is a healing force

Clear your mind and surrender to the divine beat. The drums will do the healing.

HOW TO CHANT?

Chanting, your body becomes a temple and an instrument. Respect your body signals. Are you nervous when you chant? Is your voice very quiet, are you afraid to be seen or heard? Is your throat too tight? Are you **chanting** from your navel or from your head? Are you centered, grounded, balanced and do you respect equally the needs of your heart and the needs of your head? Are you too loud? Is your ego fighting to get in? Do you chant because you want others to hear you or because you want to become the **Divine energy** and you want to let the **Divine** flow run through you.

Module 12 Spirituality & You

Gratefully Giving & Receiving Divine Flow

Exercise 1 Have Divine as the main focus all through your day

Just before you start walking, talking, driving, just before you open a door, or start an activity, have in mind that everything is Divine, that all is One, that All is God. Put this thought consciously in front of all your activity.

You are an Instrument in God's Hands

Feel all through the day the interconnectedness of all beings, all things, all actions, all thoughts, all feelings. Remember all through the day the synchronicity that exists in all our lives. Remind yourself that you are an instrument in God's Hands, an instrument of Divine…

Divine in day-to-day tasks

One of your daily tasks should be done with love, enthusiasm and devotion as though your life depends on it. Whether you chose to clean your bedroom, wash the dishes or wash your car in this way, do it completely, engage fully, do it the best you can.

Exercise 2 Enter Your Dream World

Out of Body Awareness

Dreams are a **symbolic represent**ation of what is going on in our **waking consciousness**.

Dreams also represent the **collective unconscious** that might be common to all cultures and

Dreams are also our ability to view the spiritual world.

For **Jung**, the symbolic messages contained in our dreams are the way to integrate the **archetypal forces** into our **existence**. For Steiner, we go into the dreamtime or spiritual world in order to find our true self.

In either way, by deepening our **awareness** of dream states we deeper connect with the states that are behind our **ordinary thinking and sense perception**.

Our soul can absorb the spiritual truths during sleep. You could decide to consult your dreams or to follow your intuitive soul.

Practice Separating from your Body

The following exercise is designed to practice separating from the body.

While meditating, sitting cross legged, or laying down, imagine that your head starts turning left or right. Follow it. Feel it turning. See within your mind's eye the room changing – you are observing a left side of the room and then the right side. If you are laying down, practice a slow movement up within your imagination with the whole of your body. Then, practice slow turning around the centre within your stomach.

Dreams & Practicing Awareness

Just before falling asleep give your 'Self' an instruction to remember the dream and to become aware of the 'Self' within the dream. Before falling asleep say 'I will become conscious of my astral journey'.

If you had an interesting dream the night before, say to yourself that you wish to continue with the dream or repeat the dream you had.

Or: 'I wish to help somebody this night',

Or: 'I wish to dream of _____'

REMEMBERING DREAMS

Your Dream Diary

Now, set an alarm clock at 3:45AM and wake up to write down your dream. Put a note-book on your bedside table and when you wake up, write down the notes of your dreaming state.

Try to answer the following questions:

- was your dream in color
- did you have a beautiful dream or a nightmare
- what is the feeling you are left behind: inspired, elevated, scared, confused
- write down the dream if you remember it, or just parts of it that 'feel' important
- how active, expressive, alive were you in your dreams
- is there a message you are left with after this dream

Watch out for **powerful dreams** with intense feelings, intricate symbols and strong colors. A dream could become a spiritual force, a message from your **Soul**, if we just learn how to dream with **awareness**, or how to stay 'awake' while sleeping.

In the morning, **connect with your dream** and try to 'feel' it, its meaning and its message.

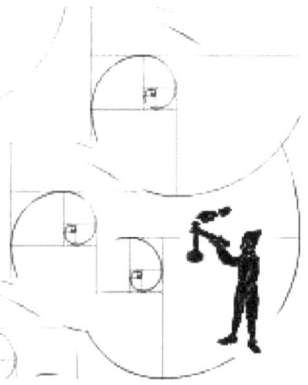

Exercise 3 Seek Spiritual Company

Once you have embarked on the journey of spiritual discoveries, you will seek inspiration from people around you – you will seek **philosophers**, **artists**, **yogis**, **gurus** and friends that will discuss spiritual topics with you.

Good spiritual books are great companions on a **spiritual journey**. Check our List of Recommended Spiritual Literature

Will and Love Practiced to invoke her Majesty Kundalini
In the world where Adepts die & bloom as Lotuses
The perfection of Union is Silence
The Desire for Beauty within a Dolphin
that possesses the Soul
keeping it under Abyss, giving It Madness of the Pan
seeking the totality of all possible 'do'-s
jumping into the river full of streams of thoughts
Until... The steady sound of a flute Stills Its Mind
Freeing it from its Grossness and Violence
destroying the illusions of shame and desires,
and loathsome forms of Ego-structures
allowing Faun to appear and Accept Its True Nature
Aiming at Perfection day after day Purging all of 'I's,
Uniting with 'All'
the Will finally becomes the Self
the Faun transforms into the Unicorn
that knows the Life of Pure Joy
and have only thoughts of clarity and splendour
Worshiping Silence Ecstasy Transcends Expression
The Soul is Freed

Alchemy of Soul by **Nuit**

artof4elements.com

List of Recommended Books

1. Tao Te Ching
2. **Patanjali** Yoga Sutras (The Light of the Soul, Alice Bailey)
3. Bhagavad-Gita (with **Sivananda's** commentary)
4. **Ouspensky**, The Fourth Way
5. **Sri Aurobindo**, The Synthesis of Yoga
6. **C.W. Leadbeater**, Invisible Helpers; Man Visible and Invisible; Chakras
7. **Powel**: Astral Body; Ethetic Body; Mental Body
8. **Shivananda**: Kundalini Yoga; Concentration and Meditation
9. Swami **Devananda**: Meditation and Mantras
10. **Avalon**: Serpent Power
11. **Krishnamurti's** Collection of Writings
12. **Aleister Crowley**: The Book of Thoth
13. **Theresa of Avila**: the Interior Castle
14. **Steiner**: How to know higher words;
15. Tibetan Book of Living and Dieing
16. **Yogananda**: Autobiography of a Yogi
17. **Alice Bailey**: The Light of the Soul
18. **C.G. Jung**: The Psychology of Kundalini Yoga
19. **Herman Hesse**: Collection of Writings
20. **Shrii Shrii Anandamurti**: Collection of Writings
21. **Makaja**: Kundalini
22. **Dalai Lama**: Destructive Emotions
23. **Osho Rajneesh**: Book of Secrets
24. Tolstoy: Collection of Writings
25. I Ching
26. Kabbalah
27. Mythology, Symbols and Signs
28. Astrology

Alchemy of Love Mindfulness Training is published by: Art of 4 Elements. Alchemy of Love Mindfulness Training consists of:

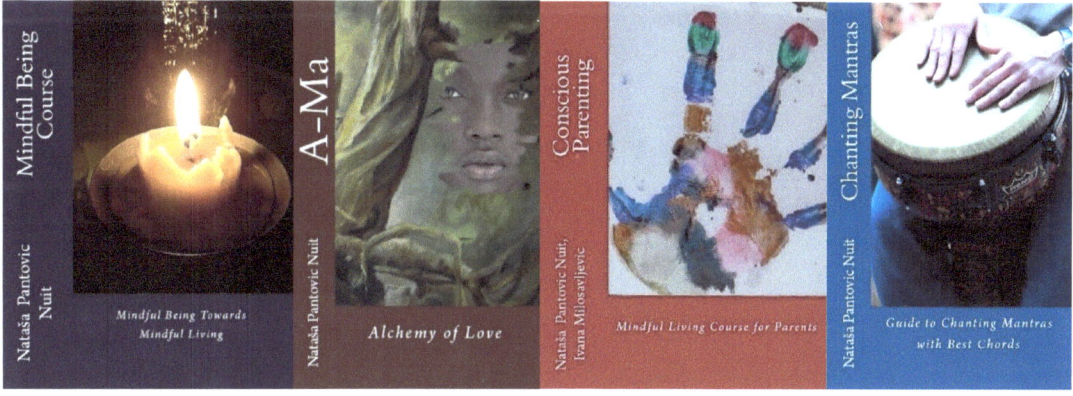

1. Art of 4 Elements, Spiritual Poetry Book, by Nataša Pantović Nuit, Jason Lu, Christin Cutajar, Jeni Caruana
2. A Guide to Mindful Eating with 45 Veggie Recipes by Nataša Pantović Nuit and Mirjana Musulin
3. Mindful Eating with Delicious Raw Vegan Recipes by Nataša Pantović Nuit and Olivera Rosic
4. Mindful Being Course by Nataša Pantović Nuit. Also available as Mindful Being Gold supported with 25 presentations, 11h video material
5. A-Ma Alchemy of Love Spiritual Novel
6. Conscious Parenting Course by Nuit and Ivana Milosavljevic, also available as Conscious Parenting Gold supported with 30 presentations, 11h video material
7. Chanting Mantras with Best Chords by Nuit

About the Author

Nataša Pantovic Nuit is a poet, a writer, and a spiritual researcher that lives and works in Malta.

Nuit has designed the **Alchemy of Love Mindfulness Training Courses**.

The Alchemy of Love Mindfulness Training is about the alchemy of love, the alchemy of soul, our everlasting quest to find the gold within, discovering the stone that transforms metals into gold.

Nuit is a poet, a writer, a Yogi and a spiritual researcher on self-development, yoga, alchemy, and higher states of consciousness.

Nuit Personal Highlights or some weird and wonderful things about me:

- BSc Economics
- I never had a TV or a mobile phone
- Traveled through more than 150 countries and lived in 5: UK, New Zealand, Holland, Serbia and Malta
- After helping to build a school in a remote area of Ethiopia, entered the most amazing world of parenthood adopting two lovely children from Ethiopia as a single mother (now imagine that!).
- My soul is the one of a nomad and during my life-time I set foot on all the continents. My home is in Amsterdam, London, Belgrade, Sliema, Rome, wherever I found my heart beating the same rhythm.
- 1991 Published my first book called: Contracts for Companies in Serbia.
- 5 years in Management Consultancy, Malta Office of the Prime Minister
- 10 years as Head of Business Development of an UK IT company
- Trainer and facilitator of Communication and Creativity Workshops in: Mindfulness, Leadership, Communication, Creativity
- 25 years of experience in yoga and meditation, 25 years of yogic life-style, a Sivananda Certified Yoga Teacher
- Organizer of 6 Body, Mind and Spirit Festivals in Malta
- Keen interest in exploring Megalithic Temples. One of the organizers of 10 days Megalithic Conference in Malta
- Regularly publish articles on Self-Development and Personal Growth
- My children are my biggest Conscious Parenting Teachers: Ema is now 12 and Andrej is 9. They love and train basketball, act within a Music Theater Group and were Chess Champions of Malta.
- Published 7 books within the Alchemy of Love Mindfulness Training

Published by Artof4elementsArt of 4 Elements is a Mindfulness Training and Self-help publisher that publishes books, audio, and video materials in areas of Mindfulness, Meditation, Self-Help, New Thought, Alternative Health, Vegetarian and Vegan Food and Nutrition, and Conscious Parenting.